OUR LIFESHIP

A study in Proverbs for Women

Lynn Wallace

Ambassador International

GREENVILLE, SOUTH CAROLINA & BELFAST, NORTHERN IRELAND

OUR LIFESHIP
A study in Proverbs for Women

All Scriptures are taken from the Holy Bible, King James Version.

Cover design and page layout by David Siglin of A&E Media

ISBN 978-1-932307-92-4

Published by the Ambassador Group

Ambassador International
427 Wade Hampton Blvd.
Greenville, SC 29609
USA
www.emeraldhouse.com

and

Ambassador Publications Ltd.
Providence House
Ardenlee Street
Belfast BT6 8QJ
Northern Ireland
www.ambassador-productions.com

The colophon is a trademark of Ambassador

Table of Contents

Acknowledgment 7
Introduction 9

Chapter 1   Watch That Helm! 11
Chapter 2   Watch That Heart! 19
Chapter 3   Watch That Tongue! 29
Chapter 4   Watch That Building! 39
Chapter 5   Watch Those Hands! 47
Chapter 6   Watch Your Companions! 55
Chapter 7   Watch Those Treasures! 65
Chapter 8   Watch With Godly Fear! 75
Chapter 9   Watch That Walk! 85
Chapter 10   Watch For Souls! 93
Chapter 11   Watch And Pray! 103
Chapter 12   Watch And Obey! 111
Chapter 13   Watch That Temper! 119
Chapter 14   Watch That Character! 127

Bibliography 135

Acknowledgment

My mother, who now resides in Heaven, radiated excitement at my writing achievements. If she were here now, she would be rooting for me. I thank God for the encouragement she offered me. My daughter cheered for me and offered to help me. I appreciate this very much.

Thanks to you work in the interlibrary loan system in the Montrose library. Without you, this book could not have been written. Thanks to those who assisted me when I phoned and asked for help concerning this book. Thanks to Mark Ziegler for the photos. Thanks to all who have encouraged me with my writing. Thanks to Sam Lowry and his staff at Ambassador Emerald for their kind words and encouragement. May the Lord bless each one of you.

Introduction

This book compares our life to a ship. We all sail on calm and rough seas. The pirates, headed by their captain, Satan, try to capsize our ships. Our Captain, Jesus Christ, helps us sail safely to the port as we consult our Logbook, the Bible, and seek Him daily in prayer.

Each chapter begins by quoting a verse in Proverbs and includes a brief introduction. It gives a modern day example of a sailor. Several examples of Bible-time sailors are set forth. Some ship-wrecked their lifeship. Others navigated well. In the next section, The Captain Calls, He speaks mainly from the book of Proverbs. The next section, Challenges Today's Women Face, includes situations we face or may encounter. It brings it down to where we live.

In the Bible text man is often used generically to indicate either a man or a woman.

As you peruse this book, I pray you may find some help as you sail on your lifeship.

CHAPTER 1

Watch That Helm!

God uses the analogy of a ship in chapter one. In verse five He says, "A man of understanding shall attain unto wise counsels." The English words "wise counsels" are translated from the Hebrew word *tachbulah*. The Hebrews used this term to refer to steering a ship.

Steering the Ship

Our life is a ship. The helm steers the ship. One who navigates his lifeship aright fears the Master. On life's seas a God-fearing person sails toward the portals of Heaven. In verse five the Hebrew word *tachbulah* comes from the word, *chebel*, a rope.[1] This rope guided the ship. God gives us wise counsels in the way we conduct our lifeship.[2]

As a sailor steers her lifeship, she gains knowledge of the Captain and His ways from His Logbook, the Bible.

This knowledge keeps her on course and steers her away from the wrong course. A wise woman chooses her shipmates carefully. She does not hang around with the pirates and the unruly. The God-fearing sailor knows that, while these pirates seek to enmesh others in their nets, they often entangle the sailors.

Stay away from the pirates. Do not follow their advice. Sailors who steer off course run into the shoals. "Thou shalt not follow a multitude to *do* evil" (Exo. 23:2). Say "No" when bad sailors entice you. Go the other way.

Listen to God. Those who hate knowledge and choose not the fear of the Lord will harvest the fruit of going the wrong way. It destroys them.

Those who heed God's warnings shall dwell safely and be quiet from the fear of evil. Even in adverse circumstances, the tempest may rage all around them, but the Captain gives an inner peace.

For example, Mr. Michael Childers left a job where he made over $20,000 a year to go to Bible college. "Oh, that I had surrendered to preach at twenty years of age," he says. At forty-five he did not find school easy. Two of his sons attended the same school at the same time.

This sailor finished four years of Bible school. Then the Lord led him to Montrose, Colorado, a town of more than 20,000 people. He pastors Faith Baptist Church and gives his heart to the Lord's work. He devotes most of his time to the Lord's work.

Pastor and Jan Childers raised five children for the Lord. His youngest son, Patrick Childers supports his wife, Joanna, while going to school. The oldest daughter, Rebecca, serves the Lord with her husband, Nathaniel Jossund, as our youth pastor. The next oldest, Pamela serves with her husband, Ben Graham, an evangelist. Mike Childers, the oldest son, serves with his father-in-law. Katie, the youngest works with Pamela's church in Arkansas, and wants to marry a pastor

When Pastor Childers went to marry off his oldest son, Michael, to Elizabeth, a visiting pastor preached on Sunday. Five came for salvation at the end of the morning service. Sailors flocked to the altar at the end of both meetings. The previous week two adults came to Christ. Before this, their young son disrupted junior church and challenged his Sunday School teacher. What shall we do? our pastor and workers discussed. Keep him coming, they decided. The people endeavored to show this boy we loved him. It paid off when the parents decided for the Lord.

My pastor returned from his trip. He baptized two of these converts, and expected to baptize three more.

The Lord did great things in our church since Pastor Childers came. Other adults made professions and showed signs of growth. They remained faithful to the church. The sailors started praying for property on which to build, more buses to run, more reached for Christ and more disciples for Him.

Women Who Shipwrecked

Jezebel—Murderess and Idolatress (1 Kings 21:3-24; 2 Kings 9:30-37)
Queen Jezebel, a wicked woman, steered her ship off course.

Her husband, Ahab, coveted a field that belonged to Naboth. He said, "The LORD forbid...that I should give the inheritance of my fathers to you."

The king came home and pouted. Tears streamed down his cheeks. Jezebel said, "Why are you so sad?" He told her Naboth refused to sell his field to him.

"Don't worry about it," she said. "I will give you this vineyard." She wrote letters to her servants. "Set two men of Belial [Satan] before Naboth. Let them witness against him and say, 'You blasphemed God and the king.' Then carry him out and stone him." This wicked sailor lied, murdered Naboth, and worshipped idols.

Jezebel's lifeship wrecked. Another king, Jehu, had her executed. "Throw her down," he ordered. They threw her down. The men went to bury her. They found only her skull, her feet, and the palms of her hands. The dogs ate her up. Jezebel tore down her ship. "Every wise woman buildeth her house: but the foolish plucketh it down with her hands" (Prov. 14:1). This wicked sailor lost her life and misguided her family.

Lot's Wife Looked Back

Lot's wife lost her chance to start a new life with her family. Abraham, Lot's uncle, rescued her when pirates took her family captive. He also recovered their possessions. However, Lot and his wife returned to the wicked city of Sodom.

After this, Sodom faced destruction for its wickedness. Lot's wife and her family lingered there. Two angels grabbed their hands and set them outside this wicked city.

The Lord said, "Look not behind you. ...Escape to the mountain, lest you be consumed."

The heart of Lot's wife stayed in Sodom. She longed for her home, her grown children and her possessions. This sailor looked back toward Sodom, an abominable city. In this she disobeyed God and turned into a pillar of salt. This woman failed to steer her lifeship right. She missed the Lord's blessings. "The blessing of the Lord, it maketh rich, and he addeth no sorrow with it" (Prov. 10:22). This woman lost all her earthly treasures. She laid up none for eternity.

Women Who Navigated Well

Esther—a Courageous Woman (Est. 4:14-16; 7:1-10)

The wise sailor follows wisdom as Queen Esther did. Understanding plus knowledge [wisdom] told her that joining the wrong crowd leads sea goers to participate in their misdeeds.

Queen Esther feared for her life when Uncle Mordecai challenged her to go before the king. For thirty days, he extended no call to her. Unless he held out the golden sceptre to her, certain death followed. Mordecai said to her, "Who knows whether you came into the kingdom for such a time as this?"

She called to the Jews and her servants. "Fast and pray for me three days." She fasted also. Then she said, "I will go unto the king. If I perish, I perish." This brave queen pled for her people. The king ordered the Jews' wicked enemy, Haman, hung. He plotted against Queen Esther's people. Mordecai replaced him. She steered her lifeship away from crags and shoals. She went before the king when he had not called for her. "The righteous are bold as a lion" (Prov. 28:1). Brave Queen Esther feared the king, but she risked her life for her people.

The Virgin Mary (Luke 1:20-56)

Mary, a devout woman, feared the Lord and kept herself pure. One day she saw an angel. He greeted her. "Hail, thou that art highly favored. The Lord is with thee. Blessed art thou among women."

Mary gasped and drew in her breath.

The angel said, "Fear not, Mary: for thou hast found favor with God." He informed her that God had chosen her to bear His Son.

She knit her brows. "How can this be?" she said. "I know not a man."

"The Holy Spirit will come upon you," he said. "The power of the highest will overshadow you. That holy thing which shall be born of thee shall be called the Son of God."

"Thy cousin Elisabeth... hath also conceived a son in her old age,... who was also barren. With God nothing shall be impossible."

Mary said, "Behold the handmaid of the Lord; be it unto me according to thy word."

This good sailor grabbed a few clothes and left for the hill country of Judea, a long trip from Nazareth by foot.

When she entered Elisabeth's home, she greeted her. When her cousin heard her, the baby leaped in her womb. Filled with the Holy Spirit, she said, "Blessed art thou among women, and blessed is the fruit of thy womb. ...As soon as I heard you, the babe leaped in my womb for joy. ...Blessed is she that believed. The Lord will do as He said."

Mary said, "My soul doth magnify the Lord, And my spirit hath rejoiced in God my Saviour." Mary steered her ship right. She obeyed the Lord. As Proverbs 11:3 says "The integrity of the upright shall guide them."

The Captain Calls

The Captain calls out in the places where seamen gather, "Get off the wrong course and follow Me. I will lead you on the right course."

When a woman heeds the Captain's call, He imparts wisdom to steer the helm on the right course. He promises, "The Lord giveth wisdom: out of his mouth *cometh* knowledge and understanding" (Prov. 2:6). Sailors who search for His wisdom, cry for it, and receive His words, will find it.

The Captain cries out in Proverbs 1:23 "Turn you at my reproof: behold, I will pour out my spirit unto you, I will make known my words unto you." However, the pirates refuse to heed this call. They shipwreck on the sandbars. He pours the Holy Spirit out upon the godly woman. He gives her the power to live and witness for Him.

Then the Captain sends out a calm upon the seas of life. Outwardly, the winds of circumstance may rage, but within the soul remains calm. The Captain calls, "Whoso hearkeneth unto me shall dwell safely, and shall be quiet from fear of evil" (Prov. 1:33).

"Ponder the path of thy feet," urges the Captain. "Let all thy ways be established. Turn not to the right hand nor to the left: remove thy foot from evil" (Prov. 4:26-27). What direction do our feet take us?

The Captain directs and delivers sailors who follow His way. He cries, "The righteousness of the perfect shall direct his way: but the wicked shall fall by his own wickedness. The righteousness of the upright shall deliver them: but transgressors shall be taken in *their own* naughtiness" (Prov. 11:5-6). None of us reaches sinless perfection in this life. The Lord seeks women after His own heart.

When a sailor strives to guide her ship in the right way, often our Captain causes our enemies to make peace. He says, "When a man's ways please the Lord, he maketh even his enemies to be at peace with him" (Prov. 16:7).

We steer our ship right when we stay in the Logbook. The Captain cries out, "He that keepeth the commandment keepeth his own soul; *but* he that despiseth his ways shall die" (Prov. 19:16). He counsels us not only to read and study the Bible, but also to do what it says.

A God-fearing sailor leads her children to follow Jesus. The Captain says, "Correct thy son, and he shall give thee rest; yea, he shall give delight unto thy soul" (Prov. 29:17). A mother who truly loves her children corrects them when they do wrong. The lack of discipline in many homes makes unruly children.

The Captain cries out, "The father of the righteous shall greatly rejoice: and he that begetteth a wise *child* shall have joy of him" (Prov. 23:24). Wise children follow when parents love them, discipline them, and train them in the ways of the Lord.

The wise sailor steers around Satan's traps. The Lord blesses all who keep their ships on course.

"Trust in the Lord with all thine heart; and lean not unto thine own understanding. In all thy ways acknowledge him, and he shall direct thy paths" (Prov. 3:5-6).

Challenges Today's Women Face

All of us sail on life's sea. How we steer the ship determines the course of our lives. Crags and shoals ensnare the one who drifts off course.

Some birth strong-willed children. How can we meet the challenge of steering these children in the right way? Sometimes, we apply too harsh discipline as I did once. Once my two-year-old broke my favorite sugar bowl. I corrected her many times, instead of once, to let her know not to behave this way. This lasted all day long. At other times, I overlooked her faults. Then I failed to teach her right from wrong. How can we strike a balance? God wants us to be consistent.

A woman goes to work to help make ends meet. She comes home tired. Her children demand her attention. Her nerves toss like a windsock twisting in the wind. How can a woman handle this situation? She needs to sit down, rest a few minutes and clear her mind. Then she can fix a snack and listen to each child's problem. In nice weather, she might plan a mini picnic. Sit on the back porch or on the lawn and talk. At other times the children can set the table and wash the vegetables for salad. While she fixes supper, they can read their homework.

The woman's boss or another superior gives her unwanted attention. She requires her job to support her family. She cannot afford to lose it. How can she cope with this crisis? Behaving, and dressing professionally and standing firm will avert many such dilemmas. She may contact someone who can help her. No job merits losing her reputation and self-respect. If her boss refuses to listen, she may want to look for another job.

What can a woman do when her husband leaves her or dies? Men on the job make more money than most women do. A single mother struggles to make ends meet. Prayer in all situations helps. She can explain her situation to her boss. She may go to the officials and ask why the boss does not pay what she is worth. She might check into an education on the side. Perhaps, she can get a better job.

Some women decide the clothes, babysitter and a housekeeper cost more than the job pays. Some choose to stay home, while others try to secure a better paying position. What can a woman do if this situation occurs? If she becomes a stay-at-home Mom, will she sit around and watch TV? Or will she seek to steer her ship right? Will she clean the house before her husband comes home? Will she spend time with her children? Will she keep a sense of humor whether she works or stays at home?

Other crags may tear up her ship: envy, harsh judgment, pride, bitterness, ill temper, and the tongue. Watch that helm!

Give the Helm to Jesus

Turn your lifeship over to Jesus. "Whatsoever ye do in word or deed, do all in the name of the Lord Jesus, giving thanks to God and the Father by him. Wives, submit yourselves unto your own husbands, as it is fit in the Lord" (Col. 3:17-18). Then you will sail on calm seas even in times of trouble.

Do these shoals and crags tend to shipwreck your ship? Is life's sea too rough to handle? Turn it over to Jesus and give Him the helm.

Endnotes

1 *Strong's Exhaustive Concordance*, pages 47 and 163, #s 8458 and 2256.

2 *A Commentary: Critical, Experimental, and Practical on the Old and New Testaments*, Vol. 2, by Robert Jamison, A. R. Fausset, and David Brown. William B. Eerdmans Publishing Company: Grand Rapids, Michigan, 1880, page 413.

CHAPTER 2

Watch the Heart!

The heart is the lifeline of our ship. It resembles the ship's motor. If the motor dies, the ship dies. "Keep thy heart with all diligence; for out of it *are* the issues of life" (Prov. 4:23). Ugly words and good words come out of the heart. The former will cause the helm to steer the wrong course.

Our Lifeline

We tend to look on the paint job and decorations on the ship. We may think, *Let me sail in that ship. What a beauty!* Are the mechanics of that ship in good shape? Is it sea worthy? Will it keep out the water? It is nice to have a beautiful ship in which to sail. What good will that do if it sinks or malfunctions? "But the Lord said unto Samuel, "Look not on his countenance, or on the height of his stature; because I have refused him: for *the Lord seeth* not as man seeth; for man looketh on the outward appearance, but the Lord looketh on the heart" (1 Sam. 16:7).

God looks on the heart—our lifeline. Does our lifeship keep out the water or do big waves splash into our ship? Circumstances, doubt, pride, upset our vessel. Faith, humility, and peace keep us afloat as we sail on troubled seas. Can we cross the Red Seas or Jordans in our lives?

When our heart does not keep right with God, it causes our lifeship to capsize. God wants to give us a new heart. "A new heart also will I give you, and a new spirit will I put within you: and I will take away the stony heart out of your flesh, and I will give you an heart of flesh" (Eze. 36:26). He gives us soft hearts.

A sailor with a soft heart hungers after the Word of God. She reads it, studies it, memorizes it, and meditates upon it. She becomes a doer, not merely a hearer of the Word. It changes her life.

Others can trust a good Christian woman. "The heart of her husband doth safely trust in her" (Prov. 31:11). She honors her husband and cares for his needs.

As she applies the Word to herself, she grows in knowledge and in understanding. The Holy Spirit in her heart aids the process. She possesses a sound heart because she trusts in the Captain of her ship.

The Captain fills her heart with joy even in the midst of sorrows and troubles. God says, "A merry heart doeth good *like* a medicine" (Prov. 17:22). A rejoicing heart aids her physical well-being, as well as her spiritual health.

When a sailor possesses a wise heart, others rejoice also. When people see her wisdom, they call her prudent. She speaks wise words from the treasures in her heart. She seeks and gains knowledge of her Creator. She guides her heart in the right way.

On the other hand, a bitter heart ends up steering into the crags and shoals. The wise woman forgives the sailors who offend her and keeps rowing for Christ. This forgiving spirit shields her from the crags of bitterness and anger.

For example, Ellen portrayed a woman with a righteous heart. When we drew names for our secret prayer pals, I drew her name. She listed her hobby as "helping others,"—an odd hobby, I thought.

Ellen lived in Valley Manor, a nursing home. She missed her husband who passed away a few years ago and now resides in Heaven. At the time, they lived in Montrose, Colorado. They ministered to the handicapped, whom they called "our special people." Chuck and Ellen taught our special class.

Every Sunday I saw these "special people" limp in or roll in on wheelchairs. Jesus Christ stepped in and redeemed some of these special souls.

It blessed my heart when Ellen went forward to pray with one of these special women. If one got noisy, Ellen quietly took them out of the service. I marveled at her patience.

I asked Ellen what she learned from these special people. She said, "We have learned that you don't just stop because you have a problem. Keep going right on.

My only daughter was born normal, but I had problems raising her without a daddy after he went to be with Christ. Ellen taught me to keep going on.

A compressed disk in her back in Ellen's back forced retirement. Though in much pain, Ellen did not complain. She depended on Chuck to get her up and down. When able again to attend her church, she testified, "When I can't sleep at night, I have more time to pray. I'm thankful."

Ellen continued reaching out to others where she resided in a nursing home.[1] Now she has met her Lord. She lives in Heaven where her beloved husband dwells.

Women Who Shipwrecked
Women in Noah's Day—Evil imaginations (Gen. 6:5-12)

Most women in Noah's day, woman with wicked hearts, steered their ship off course.

"Mrs. Noah, you are not going to get on Noah's boat, are you?" the woman taunted her. "I would leave my husband if he did anything that foolish."

"Lenora, you do not understand. My family believes in God. God said, 'Noah, build a big boat. People are so wicked that I will send rain. It will flood the earth.' Yes, I will board that boat. I do not want to drown."

"Do not be silly. It has never rained on the earth. We will not drown."

"Oh, Lenora, I wish you believed God. He always speaks the truth."

No one believed God except Noah's family. Only eight people climbed in the boat. All the others drowned in a worldwide flood. God also saved two of every kind of animal. This boat was big and could easily accommodate that many baby animals, including the dinosaurs. Noah may have housed smaller animals in cages.

God punished mankind for their wickedness "Every imagination of the thoughts of his (her) heart was only evil continually." God says in Proverbs 15:9, "The way of the wicked *is* an abomination unto the Lord: but he loveth him that followeth after righteousness." Noah's wife and her family boarded the ark by faith. They sailed and landed safely on Mount Ararat.

Herodias—adulteress, murderer (Matt. 14:3-12)

Herodias, a lustful, wicked woman, steered her ship in the wrong direction.

"King Herod," John said, "You broke the law by taking Herodias, Philip's wife." This angered the king and he put John in prison.

The king celebrated his birthday. Salome, Herodias' daughter, danced before him and pleased him. "I will give you whatever you ask," he promised her.

Herodias said to her, "Ask for John Baptist head in a charger." The king beheaded John and gave his head to Salome. Salome gave this head to her mother. Herodias and Salome chose the way of death. Proverbs 7:27 says, "Her house *is* the way to hell, going down to the chambers of death."

Women Who Navigated Well

Mary Magdalene—ministered unto Jesus (Luke 8:1-3; John 20:1-16)

Seven demons lived in Mary Magdalene's body. What hope was there for such a wretched woman? She served the devil and was dead in sin. She drifted on life's sea. Jesus said, "Ye shall die in your sins: for if ye believe not that I am *He*, ye shall die in your sins" (John 8:24). Fortunately, Mary Magdalene did not die in this state, and go to hell.

One day Jesus came along and saw her. He said to the seven demons, "Come out." They came out of her. She believed in Him, followed Him, and gave Him gifts of her substance. She watched Him die on the cross for her sins. As men laid His body in the tomb, she saw them. She came early on a Sunday morning to the tomb. When she did not see His body, she ran and told others. Then she went back to the tomb, and stood outside weeping.

Two angels sat inside the tomb. "Woman, why are you weeping?" they asked. "Because they have taken away my Lord, and I know not where they have laid Him," she said.

She turned around and saw Jesus, but she thought it was the gardener. "Why are you weeping?" He said. She said, "Sir, if thou have borne him hence, tell me where thou hast laid him, and I will take him away."

Jesus said, "Mary." She knew Him by the way He said her name. She said, "Master." Mary gave Jesus her heart. Proverbs 23:26 says, "My son, (daughter) give me thine heart, and let thine eyes observe my ways." Mary sailed safe into port.

Women at the tomb—their hearts longed after Jesus (Mark 15:40-41, 47-16:10; Luke 27:28-31; Acts 1:13-14)

Many women gathered to watch Jesus on the cross, observed His burial, and came to the tomb. Mary, Jesus' mother, called "the other Mary," Mary Magdalene, Mary the mother of James the less and Joses, Salome [Zebedees' wife], Joanna, Cleopas' wife, and others came together. They followed Jesus from Galilee. These women stood afar off from the cross and wept for Him.

Jesus said, "Do not weep for me. Weep for yourselves and your children. Hard times are coming." He prophesied the destruction of Jerusalem in 70 A.D.

The women followed His body to the tomb. They looked on as Joseph of Arimathaea and Nicodemus laid Him in a new sepulchre. Then they returned to the city and prepared spices and ointment to anoint His body. They waited during the preparation day and the Saturday sabbath.

Three days after the crucifixion these women returned to the tomb. They brought the spices and ointments they had prepared. They did not see His body there. God sent a great earthquake. An angel came and rolled away the heavy sealed stone. This angel appeared to the women. He spoke to them, "He is not here: for He is risen, as He said. Come, see the place where the Lord lay. Go quickly and tell His disciples." The frightened women fled from the burial place. Later, Jesus appeared to Mary Magdalene. She told the disciples. Her words seemed as idle tales.

Later, some of the same women joined the disciples in the upper room. This group of 120 waited for the Holy Spirit to come down and empower the church in Jerusalem. These women trusted Jesus and followed Him. "Trust in the Lord with all thine heart; and lean not unto thine own understanding. In all thy ways acknowledge him, and he shall direct thy paths" (Prov. 3:5-6). They loved the Lord and gathered with godly sailors.

The Captain Calls

The Captain calls to women today. "As a woman thinks in her heart, *so is* she." See Proverbs 23:7. Mark says it this way, "That which cometh out of the man, that defileth the man" (Mark 7:20). He names several sins and concludes: "All these evil things come from within, and defile the man" (Mark 7:23).

The Captain knows what is in your heart. He says, "Hell and destruction *are* before the Lord: how much more then the hearts of the children of men?" (Prov. 15:11). In John 2:24-25 He adds, "Jesus...knew all *men*, And needed not that any should testify of man: for he knew what was in man." He knows what you think. In 1 Chronicles 28:9 He says, "The LORD searcheth all hearts, and understandeth all the imaginations of the thoughts." The Lord looks for a woman whose heart is right with Him.

He pleads with us for understanding hearts. The Captain cries, "O ye simple, understand wisdom: and, ye fools, be ye of an understanding heart" (Prov. 8:5). A sailor with understanding discerns between good and evil.

The Captain calls in Proverbs 3:1, "Let thine heart keep my commandments." Obedient sailors please the Master. " Let thine heart retain my words: keep my commandments, and live" (Prov. 4:4). James 1:22 says it this way, "But be ye doers of the word, and not hearers only." Like a mirror, God's Word reflects our hearts. Some look into the Word of God, walk away, and forget what it says. Others linger over the words in this looking glass, apply it to their lives, and do what it says. God says that will bless such.

When we apply our hearts to understanding, the Captain promises to give us wisdom. He adds other conditions: pay attention to His Word, cry out for knowledge, and search for the treasures in His Word. This wisdom protects us from evil and leads us in the right paths (Prov. 2:10-20).

Of godly women the Captain says, "The wise in heart shall be called prudent: and the sweetness of the lips increaseth learning. Understanding *is* a wellspring of life unto him that hath it: but the instruction of fools is folly" (Prov. 16:21-22). She knows what is acceptable and edifies others. She speaks sweet words and encourages other believers.

The Captain warns against a foolish heart, one that despises the Word and rejects God. He says, "His heart fretteth against the LORD." He "that despiseth the Word shall be destroyed" (Prov. 19:3; 13:13). Their folly destroys them without a hope of eternity with God, except they repent.

"For as he thinketh in his heart, *so is* he: Eat and drink, saith he to thee; but his heart is not with thee" (Prov. 23:7).

Challenges Today's Women Face

God gave His sailors, a heart to love Him. Sometimes, the waves toss up and down. He can use us to calm those troubled hearts.

How do we react to a woman who becomes discouraged? Her heart is heavy. Do we try to bring her out of it by making jokes? In Proverbs 25:20 the Bible says, "As he that taketh away a garment in cold weather, *and as* vinegar upon nitre, so *is* he that singeth songs to an heavy heart." "Nitre" is baking soda. What happens if you pour vinegar on it? As the soda foams up, so will the heaviness in a woman's heart when you joke. In Romans 12:15 God gives us a solution: "Rejoice with them that do rejoice, and weep with them that weep." Do we empathize with them and show them we care? Then pray with them.

Here is an illustration of empathy. Once a sow grabbed my baby sister's foot. For a long time I remembered the incident as being my foot in the pig's snout. When I grew older and Mom retold this story, I knew it had to be my little sister's foot. I identified with her so closely that I put myself in her place. When we do this with a discouraged woman, God can use it to bring a calm in her heart.

Lying and deceit begin in the heart—even little white lies. Did we do something not right? This gets us into trouble. Sometimes, we plan in our heart how to get out of trouble? We choose a better course when we tell the truth and take the consequences for our action.

How can we deal with a woman who lifts up her head and pretends not to see us? Proverbs 16:5 says that God hates a proud heart. Do all the proud women lack Christ? Do some claim they have accepted Him? Pray for these proud women.

God helped me understand joy in the midst of sorrow. My friend's husband, Dr. Brown, passed away suddenly, leaving their young son behind. Mrs. Brown's face shone with radiancy at the funeral. Yet I knew she loved her husband. I did not understand. Years later, my beloved Leon stepped into the presence of his Saviour. He left me a teenage girl to raise. I cannot explain, but God filled my heart with joy while at the same time it broke with sorrow. This joy far surpasses the mirth of the world.

My friend, Marj, helps me when perplexity overwhelms me. The Lord gives her the right words. She lays up the knowledge of God in her heart. He gives her wisdom. Sometimes, she does not say what I want to hear, but what I need. She ministers out of a heart of love, not to make me feel good.

As we look back, we may remember the best times with our teens were when we cried together. Tears draw hearts closer together. When a woman has crushed our young person's heart, do we weep with her? Perhaps, they did something to break our heart, but they are genuinely sorry. As their eyes overflow with water, do we give them a gentle hug as tears run down our own cheeks?

A sense of humor always helps. It heals and is pleasant. It creates memories. My friend still laughs when she remembers the following incident. She saw a short woman throwing her paper plates into the trash through an open window. Accidentally, she threw some silverware in this garbage. Her feet were halfway up the can and her head inside as she searched for that knife. Afterwards both rolled with laughter.

Give the Helm to Jesus

Be wise. Give a soft answer and turn away wrath. Seek to obey God, serve Him, and encourage others. My daughter, "give me thine heart, and let thine eyes observe my ways" (Prov. 23:26).

How is it with our heart? Do troubles threaten to overturn our ship as we sail on life's sea? Jesus can bring a great calm as He did for the disciples.

Endnotes

1 "Her Hobby Is Helping," by Lynn Wallace. *God's Special People*, July 1992, pages 7-9.

CHAPTER 3

Watch That Tongue!

God compares the tongue to a helm. It determines the course of our lives. "Behold also the ships, which though they be so great, and are driven of fierce winds, yet are they turned about with a very small helm, whithersoever the governor listeth. Even so the tongue is a little member, and boasteth great things. Behold, how great a matter a little fire kindleth!...The mouth of a righteous man is a well of life: but violence covereth the mouth of the wicked (Jas. 3:4-5; Prov. 10:11).

Wisdom and the Tongue

The book of Proverbs contains more verses on the tongue than on any other subject. This little member can get us into a bunch of trouble, or minister grace to others.

The writer of James says one cannot tame the tongue. "But the tongue can no man tame; it is an unruly evil, full of deadly poison" (Jas. 3:8). However, if we submit to the Creator, He will give us wise tongues. Wisdom comes from Him.

The wise woman lays up knowledge by consulting her Logbook, the Bible, often. Humility and a willingness to learn characterize her speech. She guides her ship in the path of truth. She turns away from gossip and slanders not her neighbors. On the other hand the foolish woman thinks she is wise, but she knows nothing. Her mouth steers her in the paths of destruction. She gossips and hurts others by her talk.

God calls the wicked lips froward and perverse. This helm refuses to comply with God's laws. Thus it leads the ship in the way of destruction. It devises mischief continually and sows discord in neighborhoods and in churches. The coral reefs along the shore ensnare it. Soon the Creator will silence such in judgment—hell fire. Sometimes, this trap catches the redeemed. Hang around rough pirates and your speech will pick up their bad language. God warns against this wicked helm.

The virtuous woman "openeth her mouth with wisdom; and in her tongue is the law of kindness" (Prov. 31:26). She speaks the truth in love from a tender heart. She forgives those who have wronged her. However, sometimes wrong words come out of our mouths.

For example, *Oops! I shouldn't have said that.* It happens to all of us.

"Oh, Lord, please forgive me. I pray that Thou wilt overrule and keep my words from hurting another."

When I became frustrated, I snapped at my daughter in my anger. "O Lynette, I wish I hadn't said that. Can you forgive me?"

"Yes, Mom, I forgive you. Please forgive me for acting in a way to upset you."

When we harbor sin in our hearts, we lack God's strength. At times we may try to act like a Christian, but we live powerless lives. When those angry words come out, seek forgiveness right away. Then God gives us power to speak out for Him.

Little heated words creep up in our hearts, and our lips spout them out. King David set us a good example when he prayed, "Set a watch, O Lord, before my mouth; keep the door of my lips" (Psa. 141:3).

Women Who Shipwrecked

Zeresh, Haman's Wife—Murderess (Est. 3:1-2; 5:10-14; 7:10; 8:1-2)

"The king promoted me above all his other princes," Haman told Zeresh, his wife. "All the king's servants bowed and reverenced me. Mordecai refused to bow to me. I hate him."

Mordecai learned that Haman went before the king. He passed a law to rid his kingdom of all the Jews. Mordecai and his niece, the queen, were Jews. Mordecai dressed in sackcloth and sat before the king's gate.

"I cannot stand to see Mordecai at the king's gate," Haman told his wife. "The queen invited me to her banquet, but I cannot enjoy even that as long as I see that Mordecai."

"Make a gallows seventy-five feet high on which to hang him," Zeresh said. Haman built the hangman's noose.

"I thought the king would honor me," Haman said to his wife. "He forced me to honor my enemy, Mordecai."

Zeresh said, "You cannot stand before him. You will fall." The king's executor hung Haman on his own gallows. His ten sons hung upon the gallows. King Ahasuerus promoted Mordecai. This woman misled her husband and mourned for her sons. "The words of the wicked are to lie in wait for blood: but the mouth of the upright shall deliver them" (Prov. 12:6). Haman's wife found this proverb true.

Sapphira—lied to God (Acts 5:1-10)

Sapphira and Ananias, her husband, heard how Barnabas and others sold their houses and lands. They brought part of the price of their land and laid it at Peter's feet. However, they pretended they gave the full price. No doubt, this couple wanted the praise Barnabas received. Ananias came first to the temple area. Peter said, "Why hath Satan filled thine heart to lie to the Holy Ghost and to keep back part of the price of the land? While it remained, was it not thine own? And after it was sold, was it not in thine own power? Thou hast not lied unto men, but unto God."

When Ananias heard this, he fell down and died. Great fear came upon everyone who heard these things. Young men arose, wound up his body, carried him out, and buried him.

Sapphira knew nothing about her husband's death. She came in about three hours later.

Peter said to her, "Tell me whether ye sold the land for so much?"

"Yea, for so much," Sapphira said.

Peter said, "How is it that ye have agreed together to tempt the Spirit of the Lord? Behold, the feet of them which buried your husband are at the door, and shall carry thee out."

Sapphira fell down at Peter's feet and died. The young men came in, found her dead, carried her body, and buried her by her husband.

Great fear came upon the church and all who heard what happened.

No one forced Sapphira and Ananias to sell their land. No law said, "Bring in the full price." However, they lied not only to Peter, but also to God. The Captain says, "The lip of truth shall be established for ever: but a lying tongue is but for a moment" (Prov. 12:19). We break God's laws when we lie to Him—a serious matter. Sapphira's lying tongue lasted one moment. She disobeyed God by her lie, and He judged her sin.

Women Who Navigated Well

Sarah and Hagar turned from their sin (Gen. 16:1-15; Heb. 11:11)

God had promised Abram a child. Sarai, his wife, passed the age of giving birth. She came up with a brilliant idea in her eyes. "Abram, God has kept me from bearing children. Go in to Hagar. Maybe I can have children by her." The heathen practiced this, but they did not believe in the true and living God. They worshipped idols.

Abram could have said, "No, Sarah, I cannot do as the Canaanites. God promised me a child. I believe Him and will wait on Him." However, he listened to his wife and followed her wrong suggestion.

When Hagar found she expected Abram's child, she despised her mistress. Sarai spoke to Abram. She said in essence, "You did wrong Abram. Now my maid despises me."

"Sarai," Abram said, "Your maid belongs to you. Do what pleases you."

Sarai disciplined her maid harshly. Hagar fled.

The angel of the Lord [Jesus Christ Himself] found her by a fountain of water. "Hagar, Sarai's maid, from where do you come?" He said. "Where are you going?"

"I flee from my mistress, Sarai," she replied.

"Go back to your mistress," the Lord said. "Submit yourself to her. I will multiply your posterity. Behold, you are with child. You will bear a son. Call him Ishmael [God hears] because the LORD has heard your affliction."

Hagar called the angel of the Lord, "Thou God seest me." She named the fountain, Beerlahairoi, or "the well of Him that seest me." Her heart turned back to the Lord. She obeyed the Lord and returned to Canaan. She submitted herself unto Sarai and bore a son.

Abram called the name of his son, Ishmael, the name the Lord had given to him.

Sarai forgave her maid. We read of no more harsh treatment. In Proverbs 15:1 the Captain says, "A soft answer turneth away wrath: but grievous words stir up anger." Hard words to Hagar distressed her. She fled. Gentle rebuke often makes a difference.

Lydia—Merchant Lady (Acts 16:14-15, 40)

Lydia, sold rich purple cloth. She moved from Thyatira to Philippi. Paul met her at a prayer meeting by a river near Philippi. He sat down to speak with these women.

This merchant lady worshipped God. She believed in prayer. The Lord opened her heart and she listened to Paul. The apostle heard her testimony and baptized her. Her family and her servants came to Christ, and Paul baptized them.

"Come to my house and stay," Lydia begged. She said, "If you have judged me to be faithful, abide with us." Lydia heard the Word and waited for Christ. Paul judged Lydia faithful. God blessed Her children and all her house. Paul could not resist her urging and he planned to accept this gracious invitation.

However, a soothsayer came up to him. Paul cast out the demon and she came to Christ. Consequently, she lost her power to tell fortunes. This angered her masters. Paul and Silas ended up staying in a prison instead of Lydia's house.

After the jailor released them, they went to Lydia's house and comforted the believers. Then they left. The Captain said, "The mouth of a righteous *man* is a well of life: but violence covereth the mouth of the wicked" (Prov. 10:11). Lydia offered hospitality to Paul and his company. It blessed her as a well of life.

The Captain Calls

The Captain hates lies and loves the truth. He calls, "Lying lips *are* abomination to the Lord: but they that deal truly *are* his delight" (Prov. 12:22). Zechariah adds, "Speak ye every man the truth to his neighbour" (Zech. 8:16). If we speak truthfully and kindly to our neighbors, often we can make them our friends. We may win them to Christ if they do not know Him.

The Captain says, "Yea, if thou criest after knowledge, *and* liftest up thy voice for understanding; If thou seekest her as silver, and searchest for her as *for* hid treasures; Then shalt thou understand the fear of the Lord, and find the knowledge of God. For the Lord giveth wisdom: out of his mouth *cometh* knowledge and understanding" (Prov. 2:3-6). If we lack wisdom, the Lord promises to give it to us if we seek for it. Ask for this in faith.

When we study the Bible, we gain wisdom to impart to others. The Captain calls, "The mouth of the just bringeth forth wisdom: but the froward tongue shall be cut out. The lips of the righteous know what is acceptable: but the mouth of the wicked *speaketh* frowardness" (Prov. 10:31-32). Oh, may our speech be acceptable to God and profitable to men!

The Captain provides a way of escape to all who seek for wisdom. "To deliver thee from the way of the evil *man*, from the man that speaketh froward things; Who leave the paths of uprightness, to walk in the ways of darkness; Who rejoice to do evil, and delight in the frowardness of the wicked; Whose ways are crooked, and they froward in their paths....That thou mayest walk in the way of good *men*, and keep the paths of the righteous. For the upright shall dwell in the land, and the perfect shall remain in it" (Prov. 2:12-15, 20-21).

Most of us talk too much. The Captain cries out, "In the multitude of words there wanteth not sin: but he that refraineth his lips *is* wise" (Prov. 10:19). James adds, "Wherefore, my beloved brethren, let every man be swift to hear, slow to speak, slow to wrath" (Jas. 1:19).

He gave us our lips to feed others. The Captain says in Proverbs 10:21, "The lips of the righteous feed many: but fools die for want of wisdom." Do our words lift up others or put them down?

Pirates trouble their neighbors with their foul language. The Captain says, "An hypocrite with *his* mouth destroyeth his neighbour: but through knowledge shall the just be delivered" (Prov. 11:9). Wise speech delivers a godly sailor.

Gossip tempts many who call themselves Christians. The Captain cries out in Proverbs 17:9, "He that covereth a transgression seeketh love; but he that repeateth a matter separateth *very* friends." Do not tell secrets. Talebearers break up good friendships.

"Whoso keepeth his mouth and his tongue keepeth his soul from troubles" (Prov. 21:23).

Challenges Today's Women Face:

As we sail on life's seas, our tongues often get us into trouble. How we use our tongues will determine whether we hit the coral reefs or stay on course.

Mothers, do we pray for our children's marriage partners? As they grow older, do we suggest dates with popular guys? Reprove them when they make wrong choices? Remember, that date may later be a marriage partner. We can help our daughters understand by explaining the reason for not dating a boy who does not know Jesus.

What does God say about the "law of kindness" (Prov. 31:26)? Do we yell at our kids? Have we ever called them dumb or stupid? Do we nag at our husbands? This may seem easy, but it fails to accomplish the desired results. Say, "Honey, I know you have a problem in this area. [Name it.] May I help you work through it?" Often this approach works with husbands and children.

Theodore Roosevelt used to say: "Speak softly and carry a big stick." Yelling at kids makes them resentful and provokes them.

"It is the truth," some say when they repeat something about another. Ask silently is it kind? We do not have to tell all we know. The Bible says the prudent conceal knowledge (Prov. 12:23). Many women have trouble with gossip. It creates ill will. Ask God for help.

Lying is an universal sin. How can we make this sin repulsive to children? How can we deal with it effectively? If they lied about someone, make them apologize to that person. Taking their privileges away often proves effective.

What do we say if our boss is over attentive? Do we put up with it because we do not want to lose our job? Do we want to lose our husband instead? Or do we reply kindly? Perhaps, we could say something like, "Listen, this is an office. This kind of action is out of place here." Maybe a fellow worker kisses us. Do we cover it up with "little white lies"? Or do we tell the truth? "He got of control on his part. I did not encourage him." What does Proverbs 12:22 say about lying? God makes no distinction between "white lies" and other lies.

The book of Proverbs speaks much about a froward tongue. It speaks crossly out of warped thinking. We are out in public. Perhaps, we say to our husband, "Why did you put on that tie? It doesn't match your outfit." That may be true, but is it kind?

Do we ever say things without thinking what we are saying? The Bible says, "The heart of the righteous studieth to answer" (Prov. 16:28). When we fail to do so, we are like those without Christ. Many of us fall into this trap. I wrote these words on a 3"x5" card: "Set a watch, O Lord, before my mouth; keep the door of my lips" (Psa. 141:3). I try to remember to pray them every day.

Are we inclined to put our kids on a pedestal? We get a report that our child did something wrong at school. Are we inclined to say, "My kid would not do that?" Listen to the whole story and talk to the child about it.

Do we expect too much of our children? If they get a lower grade on their report cards, how do we handle it? Ask this child, do you have trouble with this subject? Perhaps, we can help at home. Talk to his teacher about it. In these ways we may get to the root of the problem. Troubles outside the classroom may make it hard for the child to concentrate. Remember, God did not create all children the same.

Give the Helm to Jesus

The tongue often gets us in much trouble. Proverbs 10:20, and 32 says it well: "The tongue of the just *is as* choice silver: the heart of the wicked is little worth. ...The lips of the righteous know what *is* acceptable: but the mouth of the wicked *speaketh* frowardness." Watch that tongue! Pray, "Set a watch before my lips."

The wise woman opens her mouth with wisdom. Let us think before we speak. Then we will utter the truth in love.

CHAPTER 4

Watch That Building!

Shipbuilders must pay careful attention. They check each seam to make sure it will hold back water. Even a tiny hole can spell disaster. God says, "Every wise woman buildeth her house: but the foolish plucketh it down with her hands" (Prov. 14:1).

Building the Ship

A wise builder follows the specs for the ship. If it is not built right, it will sink.

If he does not understand the pattern, he asks questions of others, perhaps the designer. A shipbuilder, too proud to consult others, may make many blunders.

It takes time to build a ship. Noah's ark took him 120 years to construct (Gen. 6:3). This required much patience of Noah and his family.

Noah's loving hands prepared the ship for his family's safety. He loved his neighbors, too. While he worked on the ark, he warned them of the coming flood and urged them to believe (2 Pet. 2:5).

Some parts for the ship weigh much. It necessitates a strong worker. If she has trouble at home, a pending divorce, or an illicit relationship, she will not keep her mind on what she does. A shoddy product results.

Some ships are built with seven masts. The masts hold up the sails. Our life ship has seven masts or sails.

A virtuous woman builds her lifeship with pure morals. She has strength of character. As Queen Esther, she courageously stands for the right. She avoids evil and decides the best means to do something. She is careful not to say nor do the wrong thing. Dr. Bob Jones, Sr., said, "Do right. If the stars fall, do right."

For example, Dad built the farmhouse back in 1936. I remember seeing that building with only the frame in place upon the foundation. Trained as an engineer, he did all the electrical and plumbing work.

This building excited me, when as a little child, I watched my house going up. He placed a real bathroom in this house. After we moved in, I no longer walked to the outhouse and bathed in that number three tub. Mom stopped heating water for baths on the stove. I did not walk out to the pump and prime it to fill my tin cup.

That house still stands after more than seventy years. Dad built it on a good foundation.

How are we building our lifeship upon the foundation, Jesus Christ? Do we construct it with wood, hay and stubble? Or do we employ gold, silver, and precious stones? One day we will stand before the Judgment Seat of Christ. The Captain will judge each of on how we built our lifeship. Will our building stand the test of time?

Women Who Shipwrecked

Athaliah—a murderer (2 Kin. 8:26-27; 11:1-21)

"Ahab," King Jehoshaphat said, "Let's make peace. You give your daughter, Athaliah, to my son, Jehoram, in marriage. They wrote out a marriage contract. Jehoram married Jezebel's daughter, Athaliah.

Athaliah followed her mother's bad example. Jehoram imitated his wife's bad example and died of a horrible disease.

Ahaziah, his son, now sat on the throne. His mother, Athaliah, counseled him in wickedness. Jehu, King of Israel, slew him.

The evil sailor, Athaliah, killed all her male children, but one. Then she reigned as queen over Judah. Her daughter, Jehosheba, hid the baby, Joash, in a bedchamber by the temple.

When young Joash turned seven, Jehoiada, the high priest, with the guard, surrounded this child. The priest crowned this young prince and guided him.

Athaliah saw King Joash, stand by a pillar. She called, "Treason, treason." The guard laid hands on her and slew her by the horse gate. The Captain says in Proverbs 14:34, "Righteousness exalteth a nation: but sin *is* a reproach to any people" (Prov. 14:34). Now the people enjoyed a righteous reign.

Tamar—Played the Harlot (Gen. 38; Matt. 1:3)

Judah had three sons by Shuah, his wife. He took a wife, Tamar, for his oldest son, Er. Because of his wickedness, God slew him. Judah told Onan, his next son, "Go in to Tamar and raise up seed for your brother." This did not please him. He did a wicked thing. This displeased the Lord who took his life.

"Tamar, remain a widow at your father's house until Shelah grows up," Judah said. Tamar did as she was told. Shelah grew up. This woman saw that her father-in-law did not keep his promise. He did not give Shelah in marriage to her.

Judah came to Timnath to shear his sheep, Tamar heard. She put off her widow's garments. She put on a veil, and dressed as a harlot. She sat in the way to Timnath.

When Judah passed by her, he took her for a harlot. She said, "Give me a gift." He promised to give her a kid goat. "What do you want for a pledge?" he asked. "Your signet, your bracelets, and your staff," she said. He handed them to her and committed the scarlet sin with her.

After this act, she put off her veil and put on her widow's garments. Judah sent a messenger with the kid goat. He did not find her. The men said, "There are no harlots in this place." He returned to Judah.

Three months later, Judah heard, "Tamar played the harlot. She expects a child by whoredom." He said, "Bring her forth. Let her be burnt." She sent to Judah and said, "By the man whose these are, am I with child. Discern whose these are: the signet, the bracelets and the staff." Judah admitted they belonged to him. He said, "She has been more righteous than I because I gave her not Shelah my son."

Tamar bore twins: Pharez and Zarah. Their mother sinned and God forgave this grievous sin. He included her in the line of the Messiah. In Proverbs 7:25 the Captain says, "Let not thine heart decline to her ways, go not astray in her paths." Avoid the paths that Tamar and Judah took. The Captain says that it can cause big trouble.

Women Who Navigated Well

Jochebed—trusted in God (Exo. 2:1-10; Heb. 11:23)

"By faith Moses, when he was born, was hid three months of his parents, because they saw he was a proper child; and they were not afraid of the king's commandment." Jochebed believed God when the king of Egypt passed a cruel law. Pharaoh said to his servants, "Cast all boy babies into the Nile River." Jochebed had just birthed an infant. She hid him for three months.

When he grew too big and noisy to hide, she built a small basket. Jochebed sealed it with slime and pitch. She placed her baby in it. His mother laid this small ark in the reeds by the river's bank. This sailor feared God more than the king's law.

Miriam stood a ways off from him. She watched over her baby brother.

Pharaoh's daughter came down to bathe in the Nile River. She saw this little ark among the reeds. She opened it. The baby cried. This little one touched her heart. She said, "This is one of the Hebrew children."

Miriam came to the princess. "Shall I call you a nurse of the Hebrew women?" she said.

The princess said, "Yes." Miriam left and called her mother. They rushed back to the river.

"Take this child away and nurse it for me," Pharaoh's daughter said. "I will pay your wages." Jochebed took her own baby and nursed it.

This child grew. When she weaned him, she brought him to the palace. The princess adopted her baby and named it Moses. She said, "Because I drew him out of the water." [Moses means drawn out.] God says in Proverbs 19:23, "The fear of the Lord *tendeth* to life: and *he that hath it* shall abide satisfied; he shall not be visited with evil." Jochebed feared God, and He spared her baby.

Deborah—a Wise Judge (Jud. 4-5)

Deborah trusted God to deliver her people. Because of sin, they became slaves to Jabin, the king of Canaan. God spoke to Barak, "Go against Sisera, the Captain." Deborah reminded him, "Did not

God command you, saying, 'Go to Mount Tabor. Take an army of ten thousand.'" Barak feared to do so.

The LORD promised Barak, "I will draw Sisera, the captain of the Canaanite army to you. He will come with his chariots and his big army. I will deliver Sisera, the captain, unto you."

Barak said to Deborah, "I will go, if you go." He refused to go without her.

"I will go with you," she said. "However, you will not receive the honor. The LORD will deliver Sisera into the hands of a woman." Deborah accompanied Barak, but not into battle.

They went to Mount Tabor with an army of ten thousand men. Sisera gathered his nine hundred chariots together and his army. "Up," Deborah said, "Today the LORD has delivered Sisera into your hand." Barak went to meet Sisera at the Kishon River.

The LORD gave the victory over Canaanite army. Sisera dismounted his chariot and fled to Jael's tent. She met him and said, "Turn in, my lord, fear not." The captain came into her tent. She covered him with a cloak.

"Give me some water," he said. Instead Jael gave him milk to drink. "Stand in the tent door," he said. "If anyone comes and asks if any man is here, say no."

Sisera fell asleep. Jael, Heber's wife, took a tent nail and a hammer. She crept into the room where he slept. She drove the nail into his temples. He died.

Deborah judged Israel for about twenty years. Judges five is her song of victory. God called a woman because a man was not willing to do the job. God says in Proverbs 3:33, "The curse of the Lord *is* in the house of the wicked: but he blesseth the habitation of the just." God blessed Deborah for her faith and courage.

The Captain Calls

A godly woman builds her ship by wisdom. The Captain calls, "Wisdom hath builded her house, she hath hewn out her seven pillars" (Prov. 9:1) These pillars are: wisdom, prudence, humility, patience, love, godly fear, and virtue. A wise woman hews out these seven pillars or masts.

She does not brag about herself, but humbly accepts the praise of others. The Captain says, "Let another man praise thee, and not thine own mouth; a stranger, and not thine own lips....He that followeth after righteousness and mercy findeth life, righteousness, and honour." (Prov. 27:2; Prov. 21:21) She bows before the Lord and fears Him. He gives her imperishable riches, honor, and eternal life.

A wise woman builds her lifeship so that when troubles come, it will not sink. However, a foolish woman plucks it down with her hands. She sits around the house and refuses to dust the furniture. The Captain says, "By much slothfulness the building decayeth; and through idleness of the hands the house droppeth through" (Eccles. 10:18).

A prudent woman plans her building before she acts. She guards her speech and her actions carefully. the Captain calls, "A prudent wife *is* from the LORD" (Prov. 19:14).

Her temper does not flare as others. The Captain cries, "*He that is* slow to anger *is* better than the mighty; and he that ruleth his spirit than he that taketh a city" (Prov. 16:32). When this virtuous woman feels disturbance, she takes a breather.

The Captain calls, "He that covereth a transgression seeketh love" (Prov. 17:9). Love for others hides their faults. God puts great value on such a woman. He says, "Her price *is* far above rubies" (Prov. 31:10). She honors her husband and seeks to please him.

On the other hand, an ungodly woman makes much noise. God does not flatter her. The Captain says, "A foolish woman *is* clamorous: *she is* simple, and knoweth nothing" (Prov. 9:13). Her arguing resembles the rain dropping on the roof. It is better to dwell in a tiny shack with peace. She causes shame to her husband, and refuses to follow his leadership. "A virtuous woman *is* a crown to her husband: but she that maketh ashamed *is* as rottenness in his bones" (Prov. 12:4). She spoils her life by her actions.

This woman gossips continuously. She runs around the neighborhood and tells everything she knows. She phones to her friends and relatives with the latest news. The Captain calls, "He that repeateth a matter separateth *very* friends" (Prov. 17:9). Often a pirate seeks divorce or her husband leaves her.

Such a woman gets her way by deceit. The Captain cries, "Bread of deceit is sweet to a man [or woman]; but afterwards his mouth shall be filled with gravel" (Prov. 20:17). Pirates suffer a bitter end.

"Through wisdom is an house builded; and by understanding it *is* established: And by knowledge shall the chambers be filled with all precious and pleasant riches" (Prov. 24:3-4).

Challenges Today's Women Face

Building our lifeship requires time and wisdom. A wise sailor studies her Logbook often to prepare the right materials. The Captain helps her as she seeks to build with gold, silver and precious stones.

Some mothers have sons or daughters who lost her Dad. A teenager rebels, and leaves home. She falls into sin and later regrets it. It causes rejoicing if they come to the Saviour. Do not despair over that prodigal son or daughter. Turn this child over to the Captain. Pray often for that wanderer.

Did a parent die or divorce? Did your teen leave home in anger? Then a teen supports herself the only way she can. She goes against all the moral principles her parents taught her. Consequently, she despises herself, and feels like a worthless piece of junk. The longer she lives in sin, the more calloused her conscience becomes. She sees no way out of her situation. God wants to forgive her and clean her from the inside out (1 John 1:9). If she does not know His Son, He wants to receive her. He loves her. He came to save sinners (Luke 19:10).

Past sin makes one feel guilty. Pain and sorrow consumes the soul. We may feel that way, but the Lord forgives and forgets our sin. Confess sin and leave it with the Captain. Forgive ourselves and believe God has forgiven us. Tell ourselves, "I confessed my sin. I know the Lord has forgiven me. Then move on with the Lord. He may not call to a mission field, but He calls each of us to a productive Christian life. Start by faithfully attending a Bible-believing, Bible-preaching church. This may encourage someone else. One person said, "Go and make everyday a big day." Do what you can.

Some women sit in a wheelchair. They announce a workday at your church. You may think, *What can I do?* One man sat in a wheelchair and thought this. The idea came to him, "You can cook." He prepared a big pot of stew with biscuits and a salad. They had a power saw for some construction work. He said, "Let me do that." He saw some children and put them to work carrying boards to the worksite. They asked to use the saw. He showed them how and said, "An adult must be here when you do this. Do not use the saw if I am not here." He supervised the children. Women can do the same things he did.

After my husband went home to Jesus, God called me to write. Many more rejection slips come in than acceptances. I could moan and groan about that as most beginning writers do. Some get discouraged and stop submitting manuscripts. However, God put writing on my heart. I cannot give up and quit.

From the start I said to myself, "I will get rejection slips. I know editors are busy people. Maybe they just received a piece similar to mine. They get so many manuscripts that they cannot accept them all. If an editor takes time to write, I call it an "encouraging rejection." Sometimes, I can use these with other editors to show them others liked my work. You may not be a writer, but God has a work for you to do. It may seem like a small task. Remember God said, "Thou hast been faithful over a few things, I will make thee ruler over many things" (Matt. 25:21). God honors those who are faithful.

Our husband comes home grumpy and tired. What can we do? Be sweet and kind. Fix a special meal for him. Keep his grumpiness to ourselves. Our good temper and a hot meal often helps bad moods. If he had a bad day at work, be sympathetic and a good listener if he needs to talk.

Give the Helm to Jesus

Often, we get discouraged when our lifeship encounters troubles. They threaten to sink our ship. "He that covereth his sins shall not prosper: but whoso confesseth and forsaketh them shall have mercy" (Prov. 28:13). God will give us the victory when we confess and forsake our sins.

Watch how we build that ship! We can safely trust in the Lord. He will guide our lifeship to a safe shore.

CHAPTER 5

Watch Those Hands!

Hands hold the helm that guides the ship. If it is not guided right, the ship will flounder on the crags and shoals. Proverbs 31:27 and Ecclesiastes 10:18 talk about industrious hands and idle hands. "She looketh well to the ways of her household, and eateth not the bread of idleness....By much slothfulness the building decayeth; and through idleness of the hands the house droppeth through." A wise builder employs her hands in useful service.

The Builder's Hands

God gives the ant as an example of a wise woman. "Go to the ant, thou sluggard; consider her ways, and be wise: Which having no guide, overseer, or ruler, Provideth her meat in the summer, *and* gathereth her food in the harvest. How long wilt thou sleep, O sluggard?...*Yet* a little sleep...: So shall thy poverty come as one that travelleth, and thy want as an armed man" (Proverbs 6:6-11). Have you ever watched the ants? They encounter an object too heavy for one ant. What do they do? Give up? No, they beckon other ants and together they carry big loads.

Once I spied a strange creature with two long antennas. What was it? I took a closer look. This ant carried two blades of grass twice as long as its length. Perhaps it used them in its nest. This busy creature prepared itself for the winter.

Picture a big ship with oars. Can one person manage the ship? No, several sailors row in rhythm. Together they guide the ship to its designation. One believer cannot handle all the work alone. However, if we each paddle our oars together, we will reach the goal.

Did you ever see a lazy ant? Not unless it was sick unto death or fatally wounded. If sailors do not take care of their ship, it will develop leaks and sink. If your ship starts sinking, take a lesson from the ant.

When does the ant gather food? At the time of harvest when it can find food plentiful. The Word of God furnishes our spiritual food. When the children of Israel wandered in the wilderness, they gathered manna daily. "Then said the Lord unto Moses, Behold, I will rain bread from heaven for you; and the people shall go out and gather a certain rate every day, that I may prove them, whether they will walk in my law, or no" (Exodus 16:4). Gather the manna of God's Word daily.

Some ants gathered their food in my house. Sugar ants devoured my cake. They stole my peanut butter. They nested in my blankets. They hid in my multi-colored dress. Ouch! Those little fire ants sting.

Do ants sleep in time of harvest? No, watch a colony of ants. They are busy creatures. Sleep instead of working and poverty will come. What happens if we sleep when the time comes to harvest souls? Will we reap any fruit? No, we work at it or our life bears no fruit. It resembles a ship with no food on board.

Ants are industrious, not idle. Proverbs has much to say about idle hands. It also speaks of diligent hands. "He that diligently seeketh good procureth favour: but he that seeketh mischief, it shall come unto him. ...Through wisdom is an house builded; and by understanding it is established" (Proverbs 11:27; 24:3).

My Aunt Bernice labored in her son's store until in her nineties. Then her children decided their mother could no longer handle forty-hour weeks. Though weary with eight-hour days, she refused to leave early. She did not want to burden others with "her work".

Did you ever get smoke in your eyes? God says, "As…smoke to the eyes, so *is* the sluggard to them that send him" (Prov. 10:26). A wise woman takes care of her things, but a lazy person wastes them. "The slothful *man* saith, *There is* a lion without, I shall be slain in the streets" (Prov. 22:13). She makes silly excuses.

For example, Mom hated magpies chattering outside her bedroom window. Climbing the spruce tree to root out their nests became an annual ritual.

At the golden age of 79 she braved a high wind as she climbed down the spruce tree. When my sister called, she related this incident to her. "Mom, you don't need to be doing that anyway," she said. "Couldn't you get someone to help you?"

"Next year I'll ask the neighbor boy to do it."

A year later she talked to my sister on the phone again. "Mom, did you get the neighbor boy to climb the spruce tree this year?"

No, I did it myself. I was afraid he might get hurt."

Often I tend to neglect all those nests of dust, and fuss that collect in my spruce tree. Then I forget the proverb that says, "The soul of the sluggard desireth, and *hath* nothing: but the soul of the diligent shall be made fat" (Prov. 13:4, KJV). Mom's example reminds me to pursue diligence in tearing out those nests. When magpies chatter, God is my hope.[1]

Women Who Shipwrecked

Potiphar's Wife—Hands Led to Deceit (Gen. 39:10-20)

Potiphar's wife paid servants to do her work. Consequently, her hands stayed idle. She supervised her servants and tried to keep her husband, Potiphar, happy. This gave her much leisure time.

Idleness leads to boredom. This woman wanted a little excitement. She gazed at Joseph, Potiphar's Hebrew slave. "Lie with me," she said.

This godly young man refused her advances. He said, "My master knows not what is with me in the house. He has committed all into my hands. Nobody is greater in the house than I. He has kept nothing back from me, but you. You are his wife. How can I do this great wickedness and sin against God?"

She did not give up her desires. She kept after Joseph day after day. He did not give in to her. He avoided all her advances.

One day when he went to do his business, Potiphar's wife stayed alone in the house. All the men worked outside. Her husband had gone on a trip. She grabbed Joseph's coat and said, "Lie with me." He left his coat in her hand, fled, and went out.

She waited until Potiphar came home. She said. "The Hebrew servant, which thou hast brought unto us, came in unto me to mock me. I lifted up my voice and cried. He left his coat with me and fled."

When she lied about Joseph to Potiphar, her husband, He believed her. In anger he threw Joseph into prison. Even there,

God blessed Joseph. God says in Proverbs 26:28 "A lying tongue hateth *those that are* afflicted by it." The master's wife hated Joseph because he refused her.

The Slothful Servant—comes to poverty (Matt. 25:26-27).

This lazy servant did not invest what the master gave him, but buried it. He gained no profit for his master.

He made many excuses. "Master, I knew you are a hard man. You reap what you do not sow. You gather where you have not scattered seed. Because I feared you, I went and hid my talent in the earth. Here, this is yours."

This angered his master. He said, "Thou wicked and slothful servant. You knew that I reap where I sowed not, and gather where I have not sown. If you had put my money to the exchangers, I would have received it with interest."

Then he said, "Take his talent. Give it to him who has ten talents." A lazy man loses even what he has. In Proverbs 24:30-34 God says, "I went by the field of the slothful, and by the vineyard of the man void of understanding; And, lo, it was all grown over with thorns, *and* nettles had covered the face thereof, and the stone wall thereof was broken down. Then I saw, *and* considered *it* well: I looked upon *it, and* received instruction. Yet a little sleep, a little slumber, a little folding of the hands to sleep: So shall thy poverty come *as* one that travelleth." The lazy man lost all he had.

Women Who Navigated Well

Ruth—She put her thoughts to action (Ruth 1-4; Matt. 1:5)

Ruth, a Moabite woman, refused to leave Naomi, her mother-in-law. She left her homeland and her gods. "Intreat me not to leave thee," she said, "*or* to return from following after thee: for whither thou goest, I will go; and where thou lodgest, I will lodge: thy people *shall be* my people, and thy God my God." She embraced the true God and His people.

Ruth made the right choice. She turned from the easy path her sister took.

This sailor put her hands to work. She gleaned grain in Boaz's field. He praised her and said, "The Lord recompense thy work, and a full reward be given thee of the Lord God of Israel, under whose wings thou art come to trust." Naomi told Ruth that Boaz was a close relative.

Naomi instructed Ruth in the Hebrew customs. The procedure she told Ruth to perform told Boaz of their kinship and asked him to marry her. She obeyed. Boaz said, "Fear not; I will do to thee all that thou requirest: for all the city of my people doth know that thou art a virtuous woman." However, he said, "There is a kinsman nearer than I." Another man had the right before Boaz to buy Naomi's field and marry her daughter.

Ruth told Naomi all that had happened. She reassured her and said, "Boaz will not rest, until he takes care of this matter."

Boaz talked to the near kinsman by the gate. He forfeited his right to buy Naomi's field. Boaz and Ruth married. God gave her a baby boy. This Moabitess became an ancestress of the Messiah, the Lord Jesus Christ. God says, "The thoughts of the diligent *tend* only to plenteousness; but of every one *that is* hasty only to want" (Prov. 21:5). Ruth worked hard and reaped a reward.

Dorcas—made clothes for widows

Dorcas, a faithful Christian woman, possessed a good and honest heart.

Dorcas came to the widows. "See these clothes I have made for you. I made coats, too. Now you can keep warm."

"Thank you, thank you," the widows said. In those days widows without a family owned nothing. Women did not go to work in those days. The welfare system did not exist. Dorcas encouraged them by making clothes for them.

However, one day Dorcas died. The widows stood around her body and wept. They sent for Simon Peter. He came. "See these coats and clothes," they said. "Dorcas made them for us. What can we do now? We cannot afford to buy what we need."

Peter sent them away and knelt by the body. He prayed. "Tabitha [woman], arise." Dorcas opened her eyes. She saw Peter and sat up.

He helped her to her feet and brought her to the widows. They rejoiced (Acts 9:36-40). Dorcas cared for the poor. God says in Proverbs 19:17, "He that hath pity upon the poor lendeth unto the Lord; and that which he hath given will he pay him again" (Prov. 19:17). Dorcas brought joy to these widows.

The Captain Calls

The Captain says, "He becometh poor that dealeth *with* a slack hand: but the hand of the diligent maketh rich" (Prov. 10:4). Hard work pleases God.

"The slothful man roasteth not that which he took in hunting: but the substance of a diligent *man* is precious," the Captain says to us in Proverbs 12:27. A godly woman cares for provisions God gives her.

Have you become discouraged because you lack what you need? The Captain says, "The soul of the sluggard desireth, and *hath* nothing: but the soul of the diligent shall be made fat" (Prov. 13:4). Trust God if poverty comes. Work if you can.

The Captain says, "The thoughts of the diligent *tend* only to plenteousness; but of every one *that* is hasty only to want" (Prov. 21:5). Stop and think, *What can I do in my situation?* Avoid those get-rich-quick schemes. When you give yourself to God, and do not fear hard work, God will supply.

The Captain calls in Proverbs 12:24, "The hand of the diligent shall bear rule: but the slothful shall be under tribute." If we employ our hands in useful service, God will bless us.

The Captain cries, "She stretcheth out her hand to the poor; yea, she reacheth forth her hands to the needy" (Prov. 31:20). The virtuous woman finds ways to help those in need.

Things never satisfy man. He wants more, more, more. The Captain tells us the way to satisfaction. "Love not sleep, lest thou come to poverty; open thine eyes, *and* thou shalt be satisfied with bread" (Prov. 20:13). Then God satisfies our physical needs and feeds us on the Bread of life.

"The way of the slothful *man* is as an hedge of thorns: but the way of the righteous is made plain" (Prov. 15:19).

Challenges Today's Women Face

The hands of sailors build the ship. Their useful service rows the boat and fills it with goods. The Captain supplies the needs of diligent and godly women.

My mother suffered two strokes. After the second one, she frowned when her fingers refused to crochet. Time hung heavy on her hands. When not running errands, I read books to her. We both found this time pleasurable.

Mom enjoyed certain things. She delighted in her great grandchildren. A great big smile spread on her face when she held one in her lap. When a caregiver let her mix up the dough, her face beamed. She loved to help others. She listened to music and learned about animals on her TV. If your mother suffers a debilitating illness, find little things that make her happy.

The ladies where she lived used to exchange culinary delights. Mother loved to bake and share her treats. As I was growing up, she made most of our clothes, even our coats. One time she bought some corduroy to make a skirt for one of us girls. When she started to put it together, she noticed the nap. The pieces did not match. She bought enough for another skirt. This pleased both my sister and me. Learn to sew, cook, or make crafts. By using these "talents", you can cause others to smile. Wherein do we find delight? Wash the dishes and sweep the floors. Your husband may not say much, but he likes a clean house. He comes home hungry. Your hands sit folded in your lap as you watch TV. How does he react? By a little effort, we can keep our honey happy.

Teach kids diligence by setting a good example. When they see Mom trying hard to keep the house in order, she may find it easier to train good helpers.

The virtuous woman cares for the poor and needy. Are their clothes threadbare? She sews or buys clothes for them. Do the children go hungry? She takes of her bounty and shares with them. She may offer to babysit while their expectant mother gets a much-needed rest. Does a mother have a child with severe physical problems? The mother's back hurts from lifting him. The godly sailor may take time to learn how to care for him. Then she can offer some relief.

Show children they are important. By actions say you care about them and love them. When small, hold them in your lap and read to them. Sit next to your teen. Weep with her; laugh with her. She may even enjoy a hug in private.

How do you celebrate the holidays? Build special memories for your kids. One Grandma still bakes special cookies for her kids. They want the decorated sugar cookies and snowballs every year. Some kids like gingerbread men. What do your kids like? Try to please them, and you will make your kids happy.

Sometimes when we shop, we find it hard to be a good steward. How much do I have to spend? Do I really need this? What gift will make that special birthday person happy and still not cost too much? Do you consider the gifts to your church? Or is giving just an afterthought? Plan and make a budget.

Fold your hands in prayer every day. Pray heartfelt prayers for lost loved ones and friends. Base your prayers on the Scriptures.

Does a neighbor need a walk shoveled or a lawn raked? You may have a neighbor who cannot get outside. How can you help her?

Sometimes, we may not be aware of the needs of others. I saw my neighbor using a walker. I baked some cookies and took them over. The family members said, "Thank you." I had enough left for another neighbor and took over some cookies. His wife said, "Bob wanted some cookies. I gave him some store cookies." God allowed me to take care of this desire when I knew nothing of it.

Give the Helm to Jesus:

Our hands can do either good or ill. "Withhold not good from them to whom it is due, when it is in the power of thine hand to do it. Say not unto thy neighbour, Go, and come again, and to morrow I will give; when thou hast it by thee" (Prov. 3:27-28).

God wants us to use our hands to serve Him and to help others. We can make a difference in this world in the way we use our hands to direct our life ship.

Endotes

1 "Mom and the Magpies," by Lynn Wallace. *Broken Streets*, 1996, page 9.

CHAPTER 6

Watch Your Companions!

If you sail in a ship with unruly sailors, it will snag on the coral reefs. "He that walketh with wise *men* shall be wise: but a companion of fools shall be destroyed" (Prov. 13:20). How can we escape from these bad-mouthed sailors? The Captain says, "Ask for wisdom. Then discretion and understanding will keep you. They will deliver you from evil men and women." See Proverbs 2:11-20.

A Sailor's Companions

Proverbs 2:12 mentions those who speak "froward things." What does froward mean? Such disobey God, act cross, unreasonable and wicked. It is hard to get along with them. Take the example of Nabal, Abigail's husband. God describes him as "churlish [rude] and evil in his doings" (1 Sam. 25:3). His wife calls him a "man of Belial" or the devil (1 Sam. 25:25).

Stay away from "enticing" sailors. The devil entices us or makes sin attractive to us. He uses flattery, motivation, and persuasion. He makes promises that He does not intend to keep. In all of this he uses people. Beware!

A violent person lures others into doing drastic things. He leads them into wrong paths and plans evil things. He speaks to accomplish his wicked plans. Avoid violent and angry people.

Asaph, a musician in the temple service, envied sinners. In Psalm 73:3 he says, "For I was envious at the foolish, *when* I saw the prosperity of the wicked." These ungodly people seemed to have it all. Then he went into the sanctuary of God, and understood their end. The Lord casts them down to everlasting destruction. Terrors consume them.

Today we observe people who leave God out of their lives. Many are wealthy. They own houses and lands. They travel in mini-homes or pull a boat behind them on a trailer. We may be tempted to envy them. God tells us not to envy sinners. Pray for them as they travel the broad way that leads to destruction.

The wise woman runs around with wise sailors. She fears the Lord, and honors her husband. She does not shun hard work and avoids the paths of the wicked. She cares for her life-ship and builds it up. If she discovers a leak, she fixes it.

For example, when we served as missionaries to the Navajo Indian, Alma became our good friend. She lived in China Springs, a few miles from Gallup, New Mexico. She built her one-room cottage of cinder blocks herself. Next door, her brother, Mark squatted in his mini-shack. He mumbled in poor Navajo. Alma spoke to him with her hands.

"Oh," she said, "I wish I knew how to tell Mark about Jesus." He "heard" only the language of her hands.

A few yards away lay black, tarpaper shacks. In these her relatives lived and drank strong drink. Alma witnessed to them of her Saviour who can take away the desire for strong drink. "Shut up," they said, "We don't want to hear your Jesus' talk." Our friend loved Jesus and did not give up. She opened her Navajo Bible and pled with her loved ones.

They strutted over to the medicine man. "Put a curse on Alma," they said. "She troubles us with her talk about Jesus."

Alma visited us often. She said, "My people hate me because I tell them about Jesus. The medicine man put a curse on me." She held up her skirt. "See this feather! The medicine man cut a hole in my skirt. It shows I'm under a curse. But I'm not afraid of his bad medicine. Jesus is greater than evil spirits."

Alma became a good friend to us because she loved Jesus and trusted Him to take of her. She befriended us because we came to tell her people of Jesus. Beware of those bad sailors and choose friends like Alma.

Women Who Shipwrecked

Maachah—idolater (1 Kings 15:2-13; 2 Chr. 11:18-19; 2 Chr. 15:16).

Maachah, King Asa's grandmother, made an idol in a grove of trees, the place of idol worship. As queen, she advised the king.

Her husband, Rehoboam, when established in his kingdom, forsook God's law. He led all Israel in this. No doubt, his wives, including Maachah, followed him in this.

This king made Maashah's son, Abijah, ruler next to himself. This made her the queen. When her son became king, she remained as his queen-adviser.

Abijah died. His son, Asa, reigned. This king removed Maachah as queen because of her idol. He cut down her idol, stamped it, and burnt it at the brook Kidron—total destruction.

Now this wicked queen lost her glory. Even those closest to us can lead us into sin. Asa did a hard thing but the right thing. God says in Proverbs 29:2 "When the righteous are in authority, the people rejoice: but when the wicked beareth rule, the people mourn." The people rejoiced when King Asa put down this wicked queen. They mourned when kings followed her advice.

Dinah—chose the wrong crowd (Gen. 34:1-2)

Dinah, Jacob's only daughter, wanted other girls for friends. However, the Canaanite girls bowed down to idols. They prostituted themselves in the worship of their gods. Dinah did not belong among these bad sailors. Dinah's people, Hebrews, worshipped the true God.

She did an unwise thing. In order to find friends, she trekked out to see these heathen girls. This caused Dinah to fall in a trap. Shechem saw her and defiled her. She disgraced not only herself, but also her entire family. "Enter not into the path of the wicked, and go not in the way of evil *men*. Avoid it, pass not by it, turn from it, and pass away" (Prov. 4:14-15). Jacob, her father, had taught her not to run around with these people. Dinah knew better than mixing with the Canaanites. She ignored Dad's wise advice and found trouble.

Women Who Navigated Well

The Shunamite Woman—hospitable (2 Kings 4:8-37)

Elisha, the man of God, passed by the Shunamite's house often. He enjoyed eating and fellowshipping with her and her husband.

She said to her husband. "This is a man of God who always goes by us. Let us make a little room for him on the wall. Let us set for him there a bed, a table, a stool, and a candlestick. Then he will have a place to stay when he visits us."

Elisha appreciated this woman. He said to Gehazi, his servant, "What can we do for her?"

Gehazi said, "She has no child. Her husband is old."

Elisha called for her. He said, "According to the time of life, you shall bear a son." She birthed a boy at the time Elisha said.

However, one day this child suffered from a heat stroke and died. The mother of the child laid his body on Elisha's bed. She went out and shut the door. She called her husband and said, "Send me one of the young men and a donkey that I may run to Elisha."

"Why go to him?" he asked.

She said, "It will be well." She saddled an donkey and said to her servant, "Do not slack up on your driving unless I tell you."

She came to Mount Carmel where Elisha was. He saw her afar off. He said to Gehazi, "There is the Shunamite woman. Run and meet her. Ask, 'Is it well with you and your husband? Is it well with the child?'"

She said, "It is well."

She came to Elisha and caught him by his feet. Gehazi started to thurst her away. The man of God said, "Let her alone. Her soul is vexed and the LORD hath hid it from me."

"Did I not desire a son of my husband?" she said. "Did I not say, do not deceive me?"

Elisha sent Gehazi to her place. He said, "Do not stop for anyone. Lay my staff upon the child's face."

The woman said, "As the Lord liveth, and as thy soul liveth, I will not leave thee." The man of God arose, and followed her. He went to his room and saw the dead child. After putting himself upon the child and stretching upon him two times, he revived. His mother showed respect to Elisha. Then she left with her child. This woman blessed Elisha. The prophet blessed her. It happened as God says, "A gracious woman retaineth honour" (Prov. 11:16).

Abigail—averted disaster (1 Sam. 25:3-38)

Nabal, Abigail's husband, sheared his sheep in Carmel. David heard about this. He sent ten young men to greet him. He said, "Say to him, 'Peace be to you and your house. Peace to all you have."

"I heard you have shearers. We have not hurt your shepherds. They missed nothing. Let these young men find favor in your sight. Give to us, we pray, and to David."

Nabal answered, "Who is David? ...Many servants break away from their master. Shall I take my bread, water and meat for my shearers and give it to men whom I do not know."

The young men came back to David. They told him what Nabal said. David said, "Put on every man his sword." Four hundred men went with David. Two hundred stayed by the stuff.

One of them told Nabal's wife what he had said. The man said, "Consider what you should do. No one can speak to Nabal, a man of Belial."

Abigail scurried. She took two hundred loaves, two bottles of wine [grape juice], five sheep ready dressed, five measures of parched corn, an hundred clusters of raisins, and two hundred cakes of figs. She laid them on donkeys. She sent servants before her and rode a donkey to Carmel. She said nothing to her husband.

She met David and his men. She said, "Let Nabal's sin be on me. He is a man of Belial [the devil]. Folly is with him. I did not see the young men whom you sent. Now the Lord hath withheld you from shedding blood. This blessing, which your handmaid hath brought, let it be given unto the young men." She brought a present to David and kept him from avenging himself for Nabal's harsh treatment. God Himself took care of Nabal.

God said of Abigail, "She is a woman of good understanding, and of a beautiful countenance." God says in Proverbs 10:13 "In the lips of him that hath understanding wisdom is found: but a rod is for the back of him that is void of understanding." Abigail showed wisdom and God used her to avert disaster.

The Captain Calls

Ungodly sailors threaten to destroy your ship. The Captain calls, "My son, walk not thou in the way with them; refrain thy foot from their path" (Prov. 1:15) Wise women will steer away from them and seek to protect their children from this unruly bunch.

The Captain says, "A companion of fools shall be destroyed" (Prov. 13:20). Whom does God call a fool? A fool in Scripture is stupid or silly, conceited, reckless and ignorant of God. The Lord talks much about these foolish sailors. He says, "Forsake the foolish, and live; and go in the way of understanding" (Prov. 9:6).

If a person does not make good sense, the Captain cries out, "Go from him when thou perceivest not *in him* the lips of knowledge" (Prov. 14:7).

A foolish sailor always seeks to bring up an argument. The Captain calls him "contentious" (Prov. 26:21). He frets against the Lord, and he utters perverse words. He tells all he knows; his speech is empty and unprofitable. God calls him proud and deceitful.

Most of us like it when people speak well of us. Many flatter others to get what they want out of them. The Captain cries out, "He that goeth about *as* a talebearer revealeth secrets: therefore meddle not with him that flattereth with his lips" (Prov. 20:19). A car salesman may tell you, "You're smart to buy that car." However, the car blows up not long after it rolls off the lot. Watch out for flatterers!

The Captain cautions us about angry sailors. "Make no friendship with an angry man; and with a furious man thou shalt not go: Lest thou learn his ways, and get a snare to thy soul" (Prov. 22:24-25). When we stay around angry people, their bad temper rubs off on us. Pray for them. Witness to them, but do not hang around with them.

The Captain warns us about playboys. He says, "The righteous *is* more excellent than his neighbour: but the way of the wicked seduceth them" (Prov.12:26). Perverts lie. Beware! They do not love you. Flee from them.

The Captain calls, "He that tilleth his land shall be satisfied with bread: but he that followeth vain *persons is* void of understanding"

(Prov. 12:11). Avoid people whose talk profits nothing. Those who run around with them lack understanding.

We see much violence today: on the TV, movies, videos, and computers. We hear it in our music. Suicide among young people is high. The Captain speaks out against the violent. "A violent man enticeth his neighbour, and leadeth him into the way *that is* not good" (Prov. 16:29).

The Captain says, "Every wise woman buildeth her house: but the foolish plucketh it down with her hands" (Prov. 14:1). The wise woman molds her household, but the foolish woman fails to care for her home.

"For the turning away of the simple shall slay them, and the prosperity of fools shall destroy them. But whoso hearkeneth unto me shall dwell safely, and shall be quiet from fear of evil" (Prov. 1:32-33).

Challenges Today's Women Face:

The Captain warns us about ungodly companions. A good sailor seeks friends who will build her up and reprove her if she gets out of line. Choose friends carefully.

My friend's place became the rallying point for the neighborhood children. She had brown kids and white kids. She had red heads, blondes and brunettes. Her "family" grew to about twelve children. She reserved two days for her family only. Now she is a grandparent and her children all serve the Lord.

Is your home a place the neighborhood kids gather? What can you do so they will want to come to your yard? Maybe you can plan a picnic for them. You may supervise games and plan fun activities. Yes, it sounds like work and will take time. However, your efforts to provide a safe haven for your kids will pay.

With whom do your kids run around? Do they have friends who get them into trouble? If you allow this to continue, their lifeship will run into the crags and shoals. Keep them away from these pirates. Explain why you do not want them around this crowd.

Invite good kids from church to your home. Is it cold and rainy outside? Spread a cloth on the floor and have an indoor "picnic". Show them how to guide their ship into safe harbors.

What will you do if a pirate asks your teenager for a date? Let your husband handle it? Okay, but what if you become a widow or divorced? What then? Tell the young person kindly to leave. Then sit down with your son and daughter and explain things to them. Help your daughter guide her ship in the right direction. If you have a son, ask him to bring his friend by the house so you can meet her. Engage her in pleasant talk. A wise sailor can tell whether she will make a suitable companion.

Sexual perverts seek to lead your daughter into sin. Sit down and talk to her about this. Warn her of the dangers. He will say, "You don't love me if you don't do it." They do not speak the truth; they do not really love her. They hunger for her body. This is not love, but lust. You might use the example of Joseph when he fled from Potiphar's wife (Genesis 39:7-12). God blessed him for his faithfulness.

Gather a bunch of young people together for picnics or camping trips up in the woods. You will enjoy this outing. It provides an excellent way for young people to get acquainted without dating.

Your teenager finds a job. The boss throws a party. It sounds like fun to your daughter. However, they will serve strong drinks. This is an adult party. How can we handle this? Sit down with our daughters and explain why we cannot approve. If she rebels, find someone who can help you.

A teenage girl lives near your house. She watches occult movies. Her parents curse and swear. You do not trust her stepfather. Explain to your teenager why this girl does not make good company. Tell her you do not want her to go over there.

Your church runs a bus route. The bus kids show disrespect to their elders around other children. If your child tells you of this situation, instruct him to talk kindly to these children about respecting elders. You may act out an example of how to do this.

A woman's husband is color-blind. She helps him pick clothes that go together, rather than laughing at him because his socks do not match. He may pick out a pair of slacks or a suit. She finds a shirt, socks and tie on occasion to compliment his outfit. He appreciates her help.

A Christian mother has a zealous son. He witnessed to a boy from another church. He said, "Mary is a sinner like us. You should not pray to her." This angered his mother. She fussed at the other boy's mother. How can we handle this situation? This Christian mother went to the other mother. In a gentle manner she explained the situation and apologized for her son. She talked to her son about tact, but did not discourage him from witnessing.

Give the Helm to Jesus:

Avoid the paths of the wicked. If you have children at home, teach them to watch their companions and to walk in the way of the Lord. Proverbs 1:10 says, "My son, if sinners entice thee, consent thou not." Instruct your children to stay away from bad companions. Use anecdotes to show them how they can get them into trouble. Widows and divorcees get advice from your pastor or someone with experience.

Do you have unruly friends? Do they threaten to overturn your ship? Look to the Lord for wisdom in dealing with them. Be wise and gain godly companions.

CHAPTER 7

Watch Those Treasures!

Our life-ship carries our treasures. "The slothful man roasteth not that which he took in hunting: but the substance of a diligent *man* is precious" (Prov. 12:27). Guard those treasures and lay them up in Heaven. These durable riches do and do not fade away. Thieves cannot steal them from us. Moths will not eat holes in them. They will never rust.

The Sailor's Treasures

The wise sailor takes cares of her treasures. With them she buys good building materials. She waterproofs her life-ship so that it will not sink.

She honors her Captain with her substance. When it comes in, she tithes and gives an offering to missions. She helps with other expenses when she can.

First, she yields herself to the Lord. "What shall I give?" she asks the Captain. Then in her heart she plans her giving. She lays aside this part with a cheerful and willing heart, not with an attitude, "I have to do this. Now I cannot buy what I want."

God blesses her life with all she needs. Sometimes, the Captain gives extra for her desires. She rejoices in His bountiful supply.

She has given herself to the Lord. She lets her Captain direct her life-ship. She lays up heavenly treasures. She helps in the church kitchen or nursery. She enjoys doing her part to keep the building clean. She may teach a Sunday School class, sing in the choir or play a musical instrument. She rejoices when she tells others about her Captain and hands out tracts.

When the Captain blesses her building, He makes her rich, and causes her no sorrow. "Lay not up for yourselves treasures upon earth, where moth and rust doth corrupt, and where thieves break through and steal: But lay up for yourselves treasures in heaven, where neither moth nor rust doth corrupt, and where thieves do not break through nor steal: For where your treasure is, there will your heart be also" (Matt. 6:19-21). She lays up treasures in heaven.

Those who sail in pirate ships seek treasures. Often, they raid another ship. The Captain says, "A good man out of the good treasure of his heart bringeth forth that which is good; and an evil man out of the evil treasure of his heart bringeth forth that which is evil: for of the abundance of the heart his mouth speaketh" (Luke 6:45). Watch out for those pirates! They will rob you of the good treasures of your heart. Then, like the pirates, you will get hung up on the coral reefs. When we fix our heart on earthly things, these worldly treasures bring forth evil.

If we set our heart upon heavenly treasures, we will reap rich rewards. Moth and rust will not harm our ship. Pirates cannot rob us of these treasures. Matthew 6:20-21 says, "But lay up for yourselves treasures in heaven, where neither moth nor rust doth corrupt, and where thieves do not break through nor steal: For where your treasure is, there will your heart be also."

Things can turn around for a bad sailor. Perhaps, she heard the gospel in her childhood. Someone gave her a gospel tract. She finds the tract and reads it. "Lord, I am a terrible sinner. Please forgive me. Take away my sins. Lord, Thou didst shed Thy blood for me. I take Thee now as my Saviour. Show me what to do." God will save the worst sinner. Now the Captain can start blessing her.

Then He will provide for her needs. Sometimes, the Captain even gives us our wants above our basic needs.

For example, we rushed and packed the last of our treasures. We loaded our piano onto the back of a U-Haul trailer. We moved them from Page to a mini storage unit. *After a year*, we thought, *we can come back and enjoy our possessions again.*

Why did we hurry so? We had to move out that day or pay another month's rent.

Where were we going? On weekends, we endeavored to build a work with the Navajo Indian. However, we discovered the Navajos took their weekend exodus, the same as white people do. We hastened preparations to go on deputation speaking in churches and thereby seeking to raise enough support to work fulltime on the Navajo field.

For six years our stuff stayed in storage. We slept on narrow mattresses, couch cushions and pads. The church gave us furniture.

At last Mom paid a mover to move our things to us. In this interval the Lord weaned my heart away from material values.

Three and one-half more years passed. On June 22, 1987, the Lord called my husband home. Soon after the funeral, I flew to Montrose, Colorado and left all my belongings behind. Monroe, my brother-in-law, brought some of my things to me in his van. He could not find my important papers, and had no room to bring my furniture. In this way the Lord continued his weaning process.

At first I lived in a small trailer and furnished it with a secondhand bed. The church and Mom provided other furniture. Later, my brother brought me a computer, and we bought a computer desk.

Through these experiences, God taught me contentment as He did Paul. Later, He gave me a nicely furnished, small doublewide for which I did not even ask. He is good to me.

Women Who Shipwrecked

Job's wife—lost treasures and gave bad advice (Job 1:- 2:10)

Her rich husband possessed thousands of domestic animals. He had a great household with servants to watch over his livestock. She birthed seven sons and three daughters. It looked like they had it made.

Then Job's wife lost everything, including her children. After this, her husband broke out with boils from head to foot. He scraped himself with a broken piece of pottery and sat down in the ashes.

She came to him. She said, "Do you still retain your integrity? Curse God and die."

Job replied, "You speak as a foolish woman. Shall we receive good at God's hands and not evil?" He did not sin with his lips.

Perhaps, Job's wife trusted too much in her wealth and her good fortune. When that was taken away, she became depressed. God says, "Better *is* little with the fear of the Lord than great treasure and trouble therewith. (Prov, 15:16). Job's wife had not learned this lesson.

Aholah and Aholibah—filled with other's wealth (Eze. 23:2-42; Prov. 2:10)

These two sisters acted the same as the strange women of Proverbs. They prostituted themselves and robbed young men of their wealth. Ornaments of fine jewels adorned them. They decked their beds with tapestry, carved works, and fine linen. Men smelled perfumes made of myrrh, aloes and cinnamon while they enriched these women.

To make themselves attractive to their young lovers, they painted their faces and decked themselves with ornaments. Men slipped bracelets on their hands and placed beautiful crowns on their heads.

They defiled themselves with idols as they cast the Lord God behind them. Their hands slew their own children and sacrificed them to their false gods. They made them pass through the fire in their pagan worship.

They corrupted not only themselves and their lovers, but they profaned the sanctuary of God with these wicked practices. They perhaps thought they could sin and get away with it. However, God said, "People shall recompense your lewdness upon you. ...Treasures of wickedness profit nothing" (Eze. 23:48; Prov. 10:2). They robbed these young men of their wealth as they paid them "the hire of a harlot". Consequently, their sin cost them their life. All their earthly treasures did not profit them.

Women Who Navigated Well
Widow at Zarephath—sacrificed for another (1 Kings 17:8-24)

The Lord led Elijah to go to Zarephath. He said, "I have

commanded a widow woman there to sustain you." Elijah left and went to this place.

He saw the woman at the gate of the city. She was gathering sticks. He called to her, "Fetch me a little water to drink."

She went to do this. He said, "Bring me a piece of bread."

She replied, "As the Lord your God lives, I have not a cake, but only one handful of meal and a little oil. I gather these sticks that I may fix it for my son and myself. We will eat it and die."

"Fear not," Elijah said. "Do as you say, but first make me a little cake. Afterwards, make for yourself and your son. For the Lord God of Israel said, 'The barrel of meal shall not waste, nor the cruise of oil fail, until the day that the Lord sends rain.'"

The widow did as Elijah asked. The three of them ate many days. The barrel of meal wasted not. The cruise of oil failed not. This was according to the Lord's words, which He spoke by Elijah.

After this, the widow's son fell ill. He died. She said to Elijah, "What have I to do with you, O man of God? Did you come to call my sin to remembrance and to slay my son?"

He stretched himself upon the child three times. He cried unto the Lord, "O Lord my God, please, let this child revive." The Lord heard his prayer. The child received life again.

Elijah carried him to his mother. He said, "See your child lives."

The widow woman said, "By this I know you are a man of God. The word of the Lord which you speak is true." By faith this woman supplied Elijah's needs. God took care of her. A severe test came when her son died. God revived him and her faith was strengthened. "Trust in the LORD with all thine heart; and lean not unto thine own understanding. In all thy ways acknowledge him, and he shall direct thy paths" (Prov. 3:3-6). This widow trusted in God and He directed her paths.

Prophet's Wife—needs supplied (2 Kings 4:1-7)
This woman's husband died owing a debt. She had no money to pay. The creditor came to claim her sons as slaves. She went to Elisha, the man of God.

She said, "My husband, your servant, died. You know he feared the Lord. The creditor has come to take away my sons as bondmen."

"What shall I do for you?" Elisha asked. "What do you have in your house?"

The woman said, "I have only one pot of oil."

Elisha told her what to do. He said, "Go borrow empty vessels from all your neighbors. Borrow many." When you come into your house, shut the door upon you and your sons. Pour out into the vessels. Set aside what is full."

She left the man of God and went home. She shut the door upon her and her sons. They brought the vessels to her. She poured oil into them. When the vessels were full, she said, "Bring me another vessel."

The sons said, "There are no more." The oil stayed.

She came back to Elisha and told him. He said, "Go, sell the oil and pay your debt. You and your children shall live off the rest."

This widow came to poverty. She almost lost her two sons. She believed in the Lord. She went to the man of God who gave her a God-directed plan. God blessed her. She paid off her debt and had enough left on which to live. God says, "He that handleth a matter wisely shall find good: and whoso trusteth in the LORD, happy *is* he" (Prov. 16:20). This widow believed Elisha, trusted in the Lord, and handled her business wisely.

The Captain Calls

The Captain says, "Labour not to be rich: cease from thine own wisdom. Wilt thou set thine eyes upon that which is not? for *riches* certainly make themselves wings; they fly away as an eagle toward heaven" (Prov. 23:4-5). If a pirate offers a bribe, refuse it. Such ill-gotten goods will flee away. A wise woman sets not her heart upon wealth. The Lord will bless her with substance.

"A faithful man shall abound with blessings: but he that maketh haste to be rich shall not be innocent" (Prov. 28:20), the Captain exclaims. The godly sailor abounds with blessings. Because she faithfully takes care of what the Lord gives her, she has all she needs and more. She avoids those get-rich-quick schemes and the disappointment they cause.

The Captain calls to this navigator. "How much better *is it* to get wisdom than gold! and to get understanding rather to be chosen than silver!" (Prov. 16:16) She falls on her knees and asks God for wisdom. An inheritance falls in her way. In Ecclesiastes 7:11 He says, "Wisdom is good with an inheritance: and *by it there is* profit to them that see the sun."

"Oh God," the woman cries, "Give me wisdom in how to invest this wisely. I want to give more to my church, and help the poor." The Captain answers, "The LORD giveth wisdom" (Prov. 2:6). God will give her wisdom, not only in her finances, but also in other areas of her life.

"Honour the Lord with thy substance, and with the firstfruits of all thine increase" (Prov. 3:9). The Captain says, God gives the increase. The godly woman pays the tithe and gives offerings.

The Captain calls to her, "He becometh poor that dealeth *with* a slack hand: but the hand of the diligent maketh rich" (Prov. 10:4). This sailor rejoices because of the Lord's blessings on her life-ship. He has blessed her not only materially, but also in other ways. She does not covet greedily after things, but knows a woman's "life consisteth not in the abundance of the things which she possesseth" (Luke 12:15). She continually receives benefits from the Lord.

"The fear of the LORD *is* my treasure," (Isa. 33:6) the Captain says. The wise sailor fears and trusts in Him. The pirates do not fear Him, but despise wisdom and instruction. They slight the Lord and His Word. The Captain says, "Whoso despiseth the word shall be destroyed: but he that feareth the commandment shall be rewarded" (Prov. 13:13). Fear the Lord and His Word.

"The Lord will not suffer the soul of the righteous to famish: but he casteth away the substance of the wicked" (Prov. 10:3).

Challenges Today's Woman Face

How will we invest it if we receive an inheritance? How will we decide? Investigate the possibilities. Consider the amount of risk we will take. What are our financial goals? Do we need a retirement income? Do we want to leave some to our children? Does our church need help above our tithe and mission offering?

Do we have property insurance and health insurance? The Lord intends for us to make plans for the future. Wise women prepare for the difficult days that may come. Has the Lord given us means of providing for the future? A wise woman will avail herself of them.

The water heater caught on fire. Call the insurance company and see if they cover damage from fire. We will pay the deductible, but they may cover the rest of the damage. What will we do if the house burns down? Stay with relatives or friends? Rent a place until the insurance pays and we buy a house? A wise woman makes plans for this beforehand.

A store calls about a bad check, but we have not shopped lately in that store. Pirates stole your checkbook and forged the signature. What can we do? Go to the bank and explain the problem. Then take the papers they hand out to the police station. This will clear the record.

If you move to an area with wool-eating moths, buy mothballs or cedar chips. Protect your woolens. Otherwise, these varmints will turn our garments into trash.

We discover mold inside our cupboards. We find out our insurance does not cover mold, but covers water damage. The water caused the mold. A good insurance calls it water damage. We hear from a company and discover the pipes are under recall. The insurance pays for all but the deductible. A wise woman has enough in her account for this. Later, the company that handles the recall sends a check for the deductible. The insurance company gets their money back. Before you have trouble, check out the insurance.

Someone vandalizes your house while you travel. What will you do? Access the damages. Call the police and be aware that they may not help. Will friends or the church help us get things back in order? What turns up missing or damaged? Make a list. You may want to spend the night with a relative or friend.

After we pay off a debt, what do we do with the money we no longer have to pay out? Why not put that money into savings each month? Next time we need a car or something else, we will not have to go into debt.

Do we attempt to teach our children money sense? How can we make them responsible for what they have? Do they respect our judgment and us? We cannot make them respect us. They respect parents who show themselves worthy.

Do we make weekly or monthly budgets? Do we adjust them from time to time? If we pay annual or semi-annual fees, do we set aside finances for these?

Do we tithe? If not, have we wondered why our money seems to have holes in it? Remember the Lord promises to bless those who take care of this. The more we give, the more He blesses (not the amount, but the proportion). Do we give to missions? The Lord blesses even more. Trust the Lord and believe His promises.

The diligent woman finds that the Lord rewards her. Those that slack off become poor. What can we do to help our present situation? How can we prepare for the future? The Lord gives us the means, but He expects us to use our heads.

Give the Helm to Jesus

Where are our treasures? A wise woman takes good care of her finances. If she lays up treasures on this earth only, she is poor indeed. God says, "The blessing of the Lord, it maketh rich, and he addeth no sorrow with it" (Prov. 10:22). We lay up heavenly treasures by obeying God.

If we love God and we love our neighbor, we will want to do right. His commandments are not grievous. Let us endeavor to take good care of our treasures.

CHAPTER 8

Watch With Godly Fear!

Good sailors fear the Lord. "The fear of the LORD *is* the beginning of wisdom: and the knowledge of the holy *is* understanding" (Prov. 9:10). How can we get wisdom? Search for it as for a treasure chest. Then you will understand the fear of the Lord. Along with it comes the knowledge of God.

A God-fearing Sailor

The "fear of the Lord" occurs often in the book of Proverbs. What does this term mean? It refers to a holy awe flowing from a godly character. Such a one loves God and shuns anything that offends the holy God. They aim at perfect obedience. While we may have perfect goals, none of us are perfect. But we strive for it in this life.

This delivers women from the pirates who speak evil things. They rejoice in doing them. It keeps her from the sailors who flatter her. She avoids their leadership in their dark and dangerous paths.

A woman who truly fears the Lord turns from her sinful ways. She seeks to please her Captain. This gives her strong confidence. It provides a place of refuge for her children. God gives her understanding.

The woman of understanding discerns between good and evil. She gains knowledge by observation and experience. This godly sailor knows her Logbook, the Bible. Wisdom uses this knowledge correctly. A wise woman thinks, speaks and acts with wisdom. She is careful in all aspects of her life.

Godly fear leads to life. It guides to a departure from the snares of death. This provides a sure and steadfast hope and anchor. Her heart finds satisfaction.

A God-fearing woman walks in her uprightness. She guides her ship aright. The fear of the Lord instructs her in wisdom. She finds honor and respect because she humbles herself before the Lord.

On the other hand, ungodly sailors do not fear the Lord. They even desecrate cemeteries and vandalize churches. One atheist pointed his finger at God. A little spider bit him and he died. Another atheist said, "If there be a God, let snakes infest my body, and my grave." Where they buried him, no snakes crawl around the rest of the cemetery. Many snakes slither around his plot.

Pirates despise the Lord and do perverse things. Lacking godly fear, they love their evil ways and lift up themselves. They boast of all their achievements. These proud sailors do not bow the knee. *Oh, how wise I am!* their arrogant hearts think.

They disregard godly wisdom and instruction. If they own a Bible, it collects dust.

Often their years are few. Sometimes, God cuts them off in the prime of life. [Some godly sailors die young. We do not understand, but we ought not to criticize them.]

Such a wicked sailor troubles his own home. He comes home in a drunken stupor and beats his wife and children. He spends all his money on drink and his shipmates lack what they need. God says that he inherits the wind.

One woman lived with her alcoholic husband fifteen years. She loved him and prayed often for him. This man came to the Lord. He gave up strong drink and started serving the Lord. Now his home became a pleasant place to live.

Pirates fall for those get-rich-quick schemes. They may surf the internet to find them. Disappointment comes when they lose the money they invested to get rich. Often, they vent their anger.

Watch out for these ungodly sailors! Leave them at the port. They do not fear God. If our company sails with them, we will end up on the crags and shoals. Welcome godly sailors. They will guide your ship in the right paths.

A godly sailor may lose a child. She feels sorrow, but does not despair as the ungodly sailors. In the face of death, she has hope of eternal life. She expects to see her child again. If widowed, she asks the Lord, "What wilt Thou have me do ?" While she waits upon Him, she busies herself with the tasks before her.

For example, the Lord took my husband home, and left me with a fourteen-year-old child. I thought, *What does the Lord have for me now?* Leon and I had planned to return to the Navajo mission field. Now, a widow, this door closed. I thought, *It will take a long time before I know the Lord's answer.*

Next week, after I lost my beloved husband, I attended his brother's church. The pastor described my shanty. He had never seen it. He spoke about writing. I knew the Lord was speaking to me. I said, "Yes, Lord, I will write for Thee." In one week the Lord answered my prayer.

Women Who Shipwrecked

Delilah—enticed and deceived (Jud. 16:4-31)

Delilah, a Philistine woman, pretended she loved Samson, a Hebrew. The rulers of the Philistines said to her, "Entice Samson, and see what is the source of his strength." They told her they wanted to capture him and afflict him. These evil men promised to pay her a big price. She coveted these earthly treasures.

Delilah said to Samson, "Tell me where your strength lies."

Samson said, "If they bind me with seven green twigs, I will become weak."

"Come here," she beckoned the rulers. "Bind him with seven green twigs." They did so. Men lay in wait for him in a room. Delilah said, "The Philistines be upon you, Samson." He broke those twigs as easily as a thread. They had not discovered his strength.

"You mocked me and lied to me," Delilah said. "Tell me how you can be bound."

"If they bind me with new ropes," Samson said, "then I will be weak."

Delilah bound him with new ropes. She said, "The Philistines are upon you, Samson." He broke these ropes as if they were a thread.

"You mock me and tell me lies," Delilah said. "Tell me how to bind you."

Samson said, "You can bind me if you weave my hair with the web."

She fastened his hair with a pin to the web. She said, "The Philistines be upon you, Samson." He carried away the pin of the beam and the web.

Delilah said, "How can you say you love me when your heart is not with me? You mocked me three times and did not tell me where your strength lies." Daily she pressed him with her words and urged him. She vexed his soul.

Then Samson told her all his heart. He said, "A razor has never come upon my head. The Nazarite vow was upon me before my birth. If my head is shaved, my strength will depart from me."

Delilah knew Samson had told her all his heart. She called the rulers and put him to sleep on her knees. They brought money with them to pay her. She called a barber who shaved off his hair. She afflicted him. He lost his strength because he broke the Nazarite vow.

She said, "The Philistines be upon you, Samson." He did not know that the Lord had departed from him. The Philistines captured him and put out his eyes.

Delilah, a wicked woman, enticed Samson into sin and he lost his strength. She feared not the Lord. She did not love Samson. God says in Proverbs 1:10, "My son, if sinners entice thee, consent thou not." Samson's parents warned him about evil women, but he did not listen. When Samson regained strength and pulled down the pillars, Delilah died, too.

Miriam—spoke against her leader (Exo. 15:20-22; Num. 12:1-15)

Earlier in her life, Miriam led the woman in praising God. She sang, "Sing ye to the LORD, for He hath triumphed gloriously; the horse and his rider hath He thrown into the sea." They crossed the Red Sea and were safe from the Egyptian army.

Years later, she and Aaron envied Moses' authority. They said, "Hath the LORD indeed spoken only by Moses? Hath He not spoken also by us?" As a woman, Miriam spoke out of place. Keeping quiet keeps us out of trouble. Jealousy crept into her heart and caused her to utter unwise words.

God heard Miriam and Aaron speak against Moses. He had given him his authority. Moses did not set himself up as a leader.

Suddenly the Lord spoke, "Come out ye three unto the tabernacle." They came out. The Lord came down in the pillar of cloud. He stood in the door of the tabernacle. "Aaron and Miriam," He called. They came forth.

The Lord said, "Hear now my words. If there be a prophet among you, I will speak in a vision or a dream. My servant Moses is not so, who is faithful in all my house. I will speak with Him. Why were you not afraid to speak against my servant Moses?"

The Lord was angry with Miriam and Aaron. He left.

When the cloud departed off the tabernacle, Miriam became leprous, white as snow. Aaron, the priest, looked upon her and her leprosy.

Aaron said unto Moses, "Please, do not lay this sin upon us. We have sinned and done foolishly. Do not let her be as one dead, as one whose flesh is half consumed."

Moses cried unto the Lord, "Please, heal her now, O LORD."

The Lord spoke, "If her father had spit in her face, should she not be ashamed seven days? Shut her out from the camp seven days, and then receive her again."

Because of her jealousy and unwise speech, Miriam stayed outside the camp seven days. God says, "If thou hast done foolishly in lifting up thyself, or if thou hast thought evil, *lay* thine hand upon thy mouth" (Prov. 30:32). Miriam failed to use wisdom in opening her mouth. It brought trouble to her.

Women Who Navigated Well

Elisabeth—believed God (Luke 1:5-7, 24-25, 41-60)

God said of Elisabeth and her husband, "They were both righteous before God, walking in all the commandments and ordinances of the Lord blameless." Because of her faith, God made her righteous. She had no child and had passed the age of childbearing.

God can do the impossible. He spoke to her husband, Zacharias, and told him, "Elisabeth will bear a child."

She conceived and hid herself five months. She said, "Thus hath the Lord dealt with me in the days wherein he looked on *me*, to take away my reproach among men." In the sixth month, she had a visitor, Mary of Nazareth, a virgin. Elisabeth and she visited three months. She knew her cousin was the mother of her Lord. She said, "Blessed are you among women."

Soon after Mary left, Elisabeth bore a son. Her husband and her named him John, as the angel had said. Many people heard of the Lord's blessing upon Elisabeth. They came and rejoiced with her. She prayed for a child and God answered. "The sacrifice of the wicked *is* an abomination to the Lord: but the prayer of the upright *is* his delight" (Prov. 15:8). God delighted to answer Elisabeth's prayer.

Hebrew midwives—feared not the king (Exo. 1:15-21)

The king called for the Hebrew midwives. "Shiphoah and Puah," he said, "When you see a woman about to give birth, if it is a man child, kill him."

These midwives feared God. They did not obey the king, but saved the men children alive. The king summoned them before him. "Why have you saved the men children alive?" he questioned them.

They said, "Because the Hebrew women are lively. They are delivered before the midwives come to them."

God dealt well with them because they feared Him, and not the king's commandment. The Lord made them houses and blessed them. "The fear of man bringeth a snare: but whoso putteth his trust in the LORD shall be safe" (Prov. 29:25). Shiphoah and Puah feared the Lord and trusted Him. God blessed them.

The Captain Calls

The Captain says, "The fear of the LORD *is* the beginning of wisdom: and the knowledge of the holy *is* understanding" (Prov. 9:10). Wisdom is knowledge plus understanding.

"The fear of the LORD *is* to hate evil: pride, and arrogancy, and the evil way, and the froward mouth, do I hate" (Prov. 8:13), calls the Captain. The godly woman loves the Lord, fears Him and abhors evil, anything that may displease the holy God. Pride and arrogance do not fill her heart, but with humility and reverence she bows before the Lord.

The godly woman may not appear beautiful as the world counts beauty. The Captain says, "Favour *is* deceitful, and beauty *is* vain: *but* a woman *that* feareth the LORD, she shall be praised" (Prov. 31:30). She fears the Lord; an inward beauty flows from her spirit.

The Captain cries, "The fear of the LORD *is* a fountain of life, to depart from the snares of death" (Prov. 14:27). A godly sailor rejoices in the promise of longevity. She looks forward to seeing her Captain face to face in that land where there is no more death.

This is a sure and steadfast hope as her Captain assures her, "Which *hope* we have as an anchor of the soul, both sure and stedfast" (Heb. 6:19). Godly woman cling to this hope.

The Captain calls in Proverbs 10:27, "The fear of the LORD prolongeth days: but the years of the wicked shall be shortened." Even doctors and scientists have observed that people who seek to please God often live longer.

"A merry heart doeth good *like* a medicine: but a broken spirit drieth the bones" (Prov. 17:22), says the Captain. Depression, worry, drugs, genital diseases, and such like shorten lives. Trusting in God, a singing heart, and living clean lengthens lives. A godly woman may, however, be in an accident that shortens or takes her life. Diseases do not respect persons. Do not judge when a believer or her children die prematurely. God is the Judge. He has a purpose in all He does.

The Captain cries, "In the fear of the Lord *is* strong confidence: and his children shall have a place of refuge" (Prov. 14:26). One child lives with her Grandma. She says, "I feel safe here." Her mother does not trust in the Lord. Now this child has a sure and steadfast anchor.

The fear of the Lord satisfies and protects from danger. The Captain exclaims, "The fear of the Lord *tendeth* to life: and *he that hath it* shall abide satisfied; he shall not be visited with evil" (Prov. 19:23). God cares for His own.

A woman who fears the Lord turns from sinful paths. The Captain calls, "By mercy and truth iniquity is purged: and by the fear of the

Lord *men* depart from evil" (Prov. 16:6). The Lord blesses those who live clean lives.

"Let not thine heart envy sinners: but *be thou* in the fear of the Lord all the day long" (Prov. 23:17).

Challenges Today's Women Face

A stranger breaks into the church building. He takes the sound system. He leaves muddy footprints on the carpets. He found pleasure in tearing up the booklets for the Christian school. What can the members do about this desecration? Perhaps, they can take up an offering to pay for an alarm system. Maybe some can chip in extra to pay for the sound system and the school booklets. Maybe an artist and a writer could get together to prepare materials to use while the school waits for booklets. Report the robbery and vandalism to the police.

How can we teach our children to fear the Lord? What methods will we use? Can we think of visual aids that might be helpful? The teaching they will remember most is the example we set before them. Let them see us reading our Bible and praying. Encourage them to pray for things they want. Lead them in prayers of thanksgiving when God answers.

Consider our speech. Do our words come from hearts that truly fear the Lord? When we sin, do we confess it; accept God's forgiveness, and go on to walk in victory?

How can a believer react appropriately when faced with those who do not fear the Lord? Getting even is not an option for a Christian. God tells us to love our enemies, to treat them well. Our old nature wants to fight back. How can we respond toward such with genuine love? The Bible says to feed them if they are hungry. If they are thirsty, give them a glass of cold water. If we see their livestock or pet in trouble, take care of it. The proper reaction will cause them to feel guilty. We may be able to witness to them. We can only do this effectively with a humble attitude, remembering we are sinners, too.

Give the Helm to Jesus

On every hand, we see total disregard for the things of God. God says, Proverbs 13:13 "Whoso despiseth the word shall be destroyed: but he that feareth the commandment shall be rewarded." The majority do not fear Him. They have no respect for the buildings that house our churches. Graveyards are no longer sacred. What can we do in such a society?

God-fearing women will stand out. If we each do our part, we can make a difference. God is able. He promised to bless those who fear His Word.

CHAPTER 9

Watch That Walk!

Walk in Scripture refers to the way we act or behave. God says, when we search after wisdom and understanding, He will give them. This will deliver us from evil men and women. "That thou mayest walk in the way of good *men*, and keep the paths of the righteous" (Prov. 2:1-6, 12, 16, 20). Bad sailors will tear up their lifeship, but those who act wisely will guide their ship aright.

Walking Right

If we walk in the light of the Word, God promises: "He layeth up sound wisdom for the righteous: *he is* a buckler to them that walk uprightly" (Prov. 2:7). A buckler is a shield that makes the darts fly away. When Satan attacks, God will make those arrows glance away from us.

God warns us to keep our feet from the path of sinners. The pirates will seek to entice us. Avoid them; turn the other way.

If we stay in the Logbook, we will gain wisdom and discretion. A discreet sailor thinks things through before he acts. When we do so, we will walk in safety and security. It keeps us from continually stumbling on rough places, from the rocks and shoals.

The wise woman walks in uprightness and fears the Lord. She is an understanding sailor. Her ship sails away from the coral reefs. It reaches the shore safely.

She may be poor, but God blesses her because she is a woman of integrity, of a good character. Others see Jesus in her.

A wise woman listens and learns from her Captain, and acts on this knowledge. She does not put herself above others, but humbly gains wisdom from them.

As a godly sailor, she has a high calling from her Commander. She seeks to follow and honor Him.

She shows concern for the sailors who do not follow His leading. She avoids their pernicious ways and points them to her Captain.

This sailor loves her God, and seeks to let His love flow through her to others. As Christ gave Himself for her, she gives up her own will to serve others.

If she slips, she may crash on the rocks. She watches out carefully for dangers she knows may be near. A circumspect sailor looks all around her to avoid any possible mishaps.

At times the seas may be rough, the waves huge, but in her troubles, God will deliver her as she trusts in Him.

For example, Rough seas come into all our lives as they did in mine. Some of these hard times came because I had not learned to trust God. I called my anxieties "nerves," and said, "I cannot do anything about my emotions."

A wise counselor quoted, "The joy of the Lord is your strength" (Neh. 8:10). He said, "Lynn, you're carrying too many burdens." Because I called them "nerves", I did not understand.

Soon after my husband passed away, the Lord drew close to me. I realized my "nerves" had flown away. God lifted heavy burdens from me. The following night my "nerves" started to return. I prayed, "Lord, please take them away." I experienced immediate relief. Since them, I am learning to cast my cares on Jesus. Though far from perfect, I no longer suffer depression.[1]

Women Who Shipwrecked

Rachel—envied and spoke rashly (Gen. 30:1-8; 35:16-19)

Rachel envied her sister because she was barren and Leah had children. Rachel spoke unwisely to Jacob, her husband. She said, "Give me children, or else I die."

This made Jacob angry. He said, "Am I in God's stead who hath withheld from you the fruit of the womb?"

Rachel gave him bad advice. She said, "Behold, my maid, Bilhah. Go in unto her. I may also have children by her." Jacob and Bilhah were not married. They committed adultery. Bilhah bore a son.

Rachel said, "God hath judged me, and hath also heard my voice." She called the son, Dan.

Her handmaid bore another son by Jacob. Rachel said, "With great wrestlings have I wrestled with my sister, and I have prevailed." She called her son, Naphtali.

Leah's son, Reuben, found mandrakes in the wheat field. They were supposed to increase fertility. Rachel said, "Give me of your son's mandrakes."

Leah said, "You took my husband. Would you take away my son's mandrakes also?" Rachel's sister bore Jacob two more sons and a daughter.

God remembered Rachel. She bore a son, and called him Joseph [He shall add]. She said, "God shall add to me another son."

Jacob took his family. God had said, "Go back to Bethel." On the way, Rachel had hard labor. As she was dying, she bore another son. She called him, Benoni, son of my sorrow. His father called him, Benjamin, son of my right hand. He welcomed his baby son, but buried the wife he loved.

God says, "A soft answer turneth away wrath: but grievous words stir up anger" (Prov. 15:1). Rachel stirred up anger when she spoke grievous words to Jacob. She died in childbirth.

Rebekah—deceived her husband (Gen. 27:1-17; 25:23)

Rebekah heard Isaac, her husband, say to Esau, "Behold, I am old. I know not the day of my death. Take your weapons, go out to the field, and take me some venison. Make me savory meat, such as I love, and bring it to me, that I may bless you before I die."

She spoke to Jacob, her son, "I overheard your father speak to Esau, your brother. He sent him to bring him venison to eat, and bless him before he dies."

"Go now to the flock. Bring me two kid goats. I will make savory meat for your father."

Jacob said, "Behold, Esau, my brother, is a hairy man, and I am a smooth man. My father shall feel me, and I shall seem to him as a deceiver. I shall bring a curse upon me, and not a blessing."

"Upon me be your curse," Rebekah said. "Obey my voice."

Jacob did as his mother said. He fetched two kid goats and brought them to Rebekah. She made savory meat. She took Esau's clothes for

Jacob to put on. She put the skins of the goats on his hands and on his neck. She gave him the savory meat to take to his father.

Jacob did receive the blessing, but he incurred the wrath of his brother. He said goodbye to his mother as he fled from Esau. He saw her for the last time as she waved to him. How much better it might have been if he and Rebekah had waited on the Lord! God had promised to give him the blessing. God says in Proverbs 20:17 "Bread of deceit *is* sweet to a man; but afterwards his mouth shall be filled with gravel." The bread of deceit seemed sweet to Rebekah, but it turned to gravel in her mouth. She never saw her favorite son again.

Women Who Navigated Well

Manoah's Wife—spoke and acted wisely (Jud. 13:1-14, 22-24)

Manoah's wife saw the angel of the Lord. He said, "Thou art barren,…thou shalt conceive, and bear a son….The child shall be a Nazarite unto God from the womb. He shall begin to deliver Israel out of the hand of the Philistines."

She came and told her husband what He said. Manoah prayed, "O my Lord, let the man of God which Thou didst send come again unto us, and teach us what we shall do unto the child that shall be born."

The angel of God appeared again to his wife. She ran and told her husband. He followed his wife to the field. He asked, "Are you the man that spakest unto the woman?"

He said, "I am."

Manoah asked, "How shall we order the child, and how shall we do unto him?"

The angel of the Lord replied, "Of all that I said unto the woman, let her beware. …All that I commanded her, let her observe." The Nazarite vow allowed her to eat nothing from the grape vine before her son's birth, or any unclean thing. No razor was to come upon his head.

Manoah offered up a kid goat unto the Lord. When the flame went up toward heaven, the angel of the Lord ascended in the flame. Then they knew He was an angel of the Lord. Manoah and his wife fell on their faces. Manoah said, "We shall surely die because we have seen God."

His wife said, "If the Lord were to kill us, He would not have received a burnt offering, nor have told us such things." She bore a son and called his name Samson. God says in Proverbs 24:3 "Through wisdom is an house builded; and by understanding it is established." Manoah and his wife built their house on wisdom and God blessed them.

Naaman's Maid—gave hope to her master (2 Kings 5:1-14)

This little Jewish maid waited on Naaman's wife. The Syrians had captured her from Israel and brought her to Syria. She believed in the true God.

Her mistress' husband, Naaman, the army captain, had led his army. He was a great man, a mighty man in courage, and honorable. However, he was a leper.

This little maid spoke to her mistress. She said, "Would God my lord were with the prophet that is in Samaria! He would recover him of his leprosy."

The king's servant told his master what she had said. The king said to him, "Go, and I will send a letter to the king of Israel." This man left with gold, silver and changes of clothes. He gave the king the letter. In it the king of Syria read, "I have sent Naaman my servant to thee that thou mayst recover him of his leprosy."

The king of Israel rent his clothes. Elisha heard about this. He sent to him and asked, "Why hast thou rent thy clothes? Let him come to me. He shall know there is a prophet in Israel."

Naaman came with his horses and his chariot to Elisha's door. The prophet sent out a messenger to answer the door. He delivered the message, "Go and wash in Jordan seven times and thou shalt be clean."

Naaman stomped his feet. He expected Elisha to come to him personally and do some great thing. He said, "Are not the rivers in my land better than all the waters of Israel? May I not wash in them and be clean." He charged away from the prophet's house.

His servants reasoned with him. "My father, if the prophet had bid thee do some great thing, wouldest thou not have done it? How much rather then, when he saith unto thee, Wash, and be clean?"

Then Naaman did as Elisha bid him to do. He dipped himself seven times in Jordan. His flesh came again like the flesh of a little child and he was clean. A little maid said, "The prophet in Samaria can heal the captain of his leprosy." God says, "A word fitly spoken *is like* apples of gold in pictures of silver" (Prov. 25:11). A little maid spoke good words. When Naaman, an army captain, sought Elisha and obeyed his directions, God healed him.

The Captain Calls

The Captain calls, "Search for wisdom and understanding, and you shall find it. ...For the Lord giveth wisdom....Discretion shall preserve thee, understanding shall keep thee: To deliver thee from the way of the evil *man*, from the man that speaketh froward things;...To deliver thee from the strange woman, *even* from the stranger *which* flattereth with her words,...That thou mayest walk in the way of good *men*, and keep the paths of the righteous (Proverbs 2:1-12, 16, 20).

"My daughter," the Captain cries, "walk not thou in the way with them; refrain thy foot from their path" (Prov. 1:15).

The Captain urges His daughter, "Keep sound wisdom and discretion: so shall they be life unto thy soul, and grace to thy neck" (Prov. 3:21-22). Discreet women think things through before they act. Then God will keep them safe and secure.

The Captain calls, "He that walketh with wise *men* shall be wise: but a companion of fools shall be destroyed" (Prov. 13:20). It does make a difference with whom we walk.

Whom do you fear? The Captain cries, "He that walketh in his uprightness feareth the LORD: but *he that is* perverse in his ways despiseth him" (Prov. 14:2). A godly woman fears the Lord, but an uncouth woman scorns Him.

The Captain advises, "Better *is* the poor that walketh in his integrity, than he that *is* perverse in his lips, and is a fool . . . Better is the poor that walketh in his uprightness, than *he that is* perverse *in his* ways, though he be rich" (Prov 19:1; 28:6). A just woman walks in integrity, with a godly character, in honesty.

The Lord will deliver a woman who walks uprightly, but the woman who follows evil ways will fall. The ungodly woman follows her own heart, but the godly woman trusts in God. "Whoso walketh uprightly shall be saved: but *he that is* perverse *in his* ways shall fall at once. ...He that trusteth in *his* own heart is a fool: but whoso walketh wisely, he shall be delivered" (Prov. 28:18, 26).

The Captain commends those who walk in truth and love. "I rejoiced greatly that I found of thy children walking in truth, as we have received a commandment from the Father" (2 John 4).

Jesus Christ, the Captain, said, "I am . . . the Truth" (John 14:6). He gave us the supreme example when He shed His life-blood on the cross to save us from sin. No greater love has any man than this.

Finally the Captain calls, "Walk circumspectly" (Eph. 5:15). Such a woman walks carefully, knowing the dangers out in the world. She knows Satan has set his traps for her. By staying close to the Lord, she seeks to avoid them. However, if she does fall, she confesses her sin, and turns her back on her faults.

"He that covereth his sins shall not prosper: but whoso confesseth and forsaketh *them* shall have mercy" (Prov. 28:13).

Challenges Today's Woman Face

How much love do we show to others? Has someone hurt us? Do we carry a grudge or forgive them? God forbids grudges; they are sin when we hold them. We find it hard to forgive those who hurt us. However, sin hinders our prayers—a high price to pay. It keeps us from fellowship with our God and fellow believers. We cannot love when we have unforgiving hearts. How will you handle this? Will you go to the person against whom you hold a grudge and forgive them?

If a daughter leaves home, chooses worldly companions, and falls into sin, what will you do? If you have grown children who walk with sinners, pray for them everyday or several times a day. It may take fasting and prayer.

Sometimes we struggle to keep our children in church. We may find it hard to guard them from worldly companions. At times, it is difficult to find godly friends for them. How can we manage this? Shelter them under the cover of a good, Bible-believing, Bible-teaching church. Ask for advice from your pastor or another godly person.

What choices do we have for schooling our children? Some choose home schooling. Others send them to a Christian school. To the rest, public school may be the only option. The school is not their parent; you are. God puts the obligation of teaching on the parents. Do we have daily family devotions? Do we pray with and for our children? Do they know we spend time in a private quiet time? How strong is our faith? If we do not have more faith than our children, how will they learn to walk with God?

Do we allow our children to make mistakes and learn from them? How do we react when the tears come down, and they say, "Mom, I really messed up at school today?" Do we browbeat them or throw your arms around them and weep with them? What do we do when your toddler draws on the wall for the first time? I gave mine a rag and some water and made her scrub the wall. When she threw a temper tantrum, my husband administered discipline. Learn to distinguish between childish actions and deliberate ones.

Give the Helm to Jesus

"My daughter," the Captain says, "Keep sound wisdom and discretion: So shall they be life unto thy soul, and grace to thy neck. Then shalt thou walk in thy way safely, and thy foot shall not stumble" (Prov. 3:21-23). If we keep the sound wisdom in the Bible, and are discreet, God promises we will walk safely and not stumble. A discreet woman wisely avoids evil. We may fall, but it will not utterly cast us down. The Lord will uphold us.

> Walk carefully. In the early 1900's a songwriter wrote:
> Look well to your cables, my brother,...
> For severed the faith strands may be,...
> Take heed lest you slip from your moorings,
> And storm tossed lie out on life's sea.
> —Lizzie DeArmond, 1900

Endotes

1 "A Cage of Nerves," by Lynn Wallace. Penned from the Heart, Vol 6, page 58.

CHAPTER 10

Watch for Souls!

The woman who navigates her lifeship well is soul-conscious. The Captain says, "The fruit of the righteous *is* a tree of life; and he that winneth souls *is* wise" (Prov. 11:30). She cares about souls and seeks to win them to Christ.

Witnessing for Jesus

As she seeks to guide her ship away from the shoals, she endeavors to help others avoid the coral reefs. This wise sailor steers away from the pirates and warns others.

Ungodly sailors go astray. Like lost sheep, they cannot find the way by themselves. When they run across your paths, you have an opportunity. Tell them of Jesus. Some may scoff, but one or two may come to the Saviour.

Sow the seeds of righteousness upon life's seas. You will reap a reward and may help troubled souls. Some find comfort. Others find a Guide. The gracious God gives us a part in winning souls to Him.

Our words, empowered by the Holy Spirit, minister spiritual health to dying souls. Tell them how you came to Christ. Mark salvation verses in your Logbook. Memorize them. Use them as you speak to women of Jesus. The Word of God has power to convict and cause lost sailors to receive your Saviour. It gives them hope of Heaven.

Many times these lost sailors encounter rough seas.

For example, the waves nearly crashed over my head towards the end of my junior year in college. My health started to break.

The Spanish exam kept me awake two nights. My boyfriend's letter became serious, "Will you marry me?"

About eight years previously, I had heard the gospel. Jeanne taught me in Daily Vacation Bible School and I believed the facts. Because of this, I thought I was a Christian. However, the Lord Jesus had not come into my heart.

Before this time, I had deep questions as a child. "Who is Jesus? Is He God or is He man?"

The summer before my senior year, the Captain brought me to the end of myself. I had nowhere to look, but up. At this time, the Holy Spirit spoke to me. "Repent, repent. Christ died for your sins. He arose that you might live. Repent, repent, repent." I heard no audible voice, but the words were as plain as if He shouted at me.

I knelt by my bed. In my heart I repented of my sin and trusted Christ as my Saviour. Peace like a river flooded my heart. My problems did not magically disappear. The Lord took care of my health problems. I passed my Spanish exam, but not with an "A". I wrote a hard letter to my boyfriend. Many years later I met my husband. Now, a widow, I pray, Lord, give me power to win souls.

Women Who Shipwrecked

Eve—disobeyed God (Gen. 2:16-17; 3:1-6)

Satan, a subtle creature, charmed Eve in the garden. He appeared in the form of a serpent. This brute did not crawl on its belly as snakes do now. Perhaps, it walked on four legs as an alligator or crocodile does.

His first approach to Eve questioned the Word of God. "Hath God said?" He uses the same tactics today. People tamper with the Word of God and change it to suit themselves. It pleases the devil when they take the blood out of the Bible.

He continued, "Hath God said, Ye shall not eat of every tree of the garden?" Indeed, God did say of a certain tree, "Ye shall not eat of it." In Genesis 2:16-17 He commanded Adam, "Of every tree of the garden thou mayest freely eat: But of the tree of the knowledge of good and evil, thou shalt not eat of it: for in the day that thou eatest thereof thou shalt surely die."

When Eve answered, she added the words, "Neither shall ye touch it." God said nothing about touching this tree.

Satan's next statement denied the Word of God. He said, "Ye shall not surely die." He is a liar and the father of lies (John 8:44).

Then the devil made a promise that he could not keep. "God doth know that in the day ye eat thereof, then your eyes shall be opened, and ye shall be as gods, knowing good and evil." Men do know good and evil, but this evil one did not tell the whole story. Man cannot do good and keep from evil.

Men and women still seek to become as gods. However, we are human beings, not gods. The only God is the Almighty God who made heaven and earth. God, the heavenly angels, and humans, whom He changed by his power, live in Heaven.

Eve looked on this fruit. Her mouth watered; the fruit looked luscious—"the lust of the eyes." She wanted to be like a god—"the pride of life." She desired the knowledge Satan offered her; it whetted her appetites—"the lust of the flesh." This reminds us of 1 John 2:16: "For all that *is* in the world, the lust of the flesh, and the lust of the eyes, and the pride of life, is not of the Father, but is of the world."

Satan succeeded in deceiving her. She plucked off a fruit and sunk her teeth in it. She ate it and tasted its sweet fruit—she sinned.

Rather than giving her husband, Adam, an example of a clean and pure life, she gave him this fruit. He ate it and knew he sinned. The first couple felt shame and tried to cover it with fig leaves—an inadequate clothing.

God sought a confession of sin from them. Instead, Adam blamed Eve. She blamed the serpent. After informing them of the consequences of their sin, God shed the blood of innocent animals. He clothed them. In this way, He covered their sin.

God had said, "In the day thou eatest thereof, thou shalt surely die." When they sinned, they died spiritually—dead in sin. Through Adam, sin passed upon all men and death by sin. Death is separation. A man who dies in his sin is separated from God forever in Hell.

Satan deceived Eve by this subtilty. His mouth poured out foolishness. God says, "The tongue of the wise useth knowledge aright: but the mouth of fools poureth out foolishness" (Prov. 15:2). Eve listened to the devil's foolish words, sinned, and died spiritually. God made her a promise to send a Redeemer from Satan's power. Christ bruised his head when He died on the cross. The serpent suffered a mortal wound. Jesus Christ defeated him. Christ died on the cross, but now He lives.

Gomer—a harlot (Hos. 1:2-11; 3:1-5)

God called Gomer a wife of whoredoms and a child of whoredoms. She worked at a dishonorable profession: a harlot or a prostitute. The Lord commanded Hosea to marry her. His purpose was to provide an example to Israel. As corrupt as our society has become, decent people avoid the places where such people gather.

Proverbs repeatedly warns young men against going to a harlot's house. Yet, he commanded Hosea to marry Gomer. God's people committed spiritual adultery. This marriage served as a spiritual object lesson to Israel. They played the harlot against God when they went after false gods.

Gomer bore Hosea three children: Jezreel, Loruhamah, and Loammi. Jezreel means "God will sow"; Loruhamah—no mercy; and Loammi—not my people. God sowed or scattered His people over all the earth because they sinned. He sent cruel nations against them; they showed no mercy to them. He set Israel aside; He even said of them, "They are not my people." He called out the Gentiles (non-Jews); He called them His people (Rom. 9:24-26).

Hosea's marriage pictures God setting aside His people. This prophet set his wife aside for many days. He kept her from serving as a harlot after they married. In doing so, he portrayed Israel abiding many days without a king nor prince, without sacrifices, without images, and without the Aaronic priesthood.

God promised to sow His people, Israel, again in their land. He will call them "Ammi"—my people. He will change Loruhamah's name to "Ruhamah"—mercy. The Jews will return one day to the true and living God. Jesus Christ will come to earth and claim the Davidic throne. His chosen people will fear the Lord and His goodness.

Gomer played the harlot before Hosea married her. Parents kept their daughters close, from following her unchaste ways. Fathers warned their sons, "Stay away from harlots; do not venture near their houses." God says, "Enter not into the path of the wicked, and go not in the way of evil *men*. Avoid it, pass not by it, turn from it, and pass away" (Prov; 4:14-15). Those who follow Gomer's ways, go astray from godly paths. These pirates follow the broad way that leads to destruction.

Women Who Navigated Well

Samaritan Woman—wins many (John 4:3-42)

The Jews hated the Samaritans. They crossed the Jordan to avoid them. However, Jesus loved these people. The Bible says, "God is love." He loves everyone, but He hates sin. He never sinned, for He is God.

Jesus became a man with a body like ours. He experienced weariness, thirst, and hunger on this earth.

Jesus went through Samaria on His way to Galilee. He became weary after He walked many miles. He sat down by a well. He knew a certain Samaritan woman came about this time to draw water from the well.

When she arrived at the well, Jesus said, "Give me to drink." Though thirsty, He desired even more to share the gospel with her.

"How is it," she asked, "that thou, a Jew, asks water from me? I am a Samaritan. The Jews have no dealings with us."

Jesus answered her, "If you knew the gift of God, and who He is who said, Give me a drink. You would ask Him for living water."

"Sir," she said, "Thou hast nothing to draw water with out of this deep well. Where hast Thou living water? Art Thou greater than our father Jacob who gave us this well?"

"Whosoever drinks of this water thirsts again," He said. "Whosoever drinks of living water shall never thirst again. This living water shall be in him a well of water that springs up into everlasting life."

The woman said, "Sir, give me this water so that I will not have to come here to draw."

Jesus knew all about this woman because He is God. He pointed out her sin to her. She did not know the Saviour. She headed toward the coral reefs. Jesus wanted to rescue her.

After He pointed out her sin, she said, "Sir, I perceive that Thou art a prophet." She tried to change the subject. Jesus steered her back to the gospel.

The woman said, "I know that Messiah comes. When He comes, He will tell us all things."

"I that speak unto you am He," Jesus said.

The woman left her waterpot and went into the city. She said to the men, "Come see a man who told all things I did. Is not this the Christ?"

The men and others followed her. They came to Jesus. Many received Him as Saviour because of the woman's words. In Proverbs 10:11 God says, "The mouth of a righteous *man is* a well of life: but violence covereth the mouth of the wicked." This woman came to Jesus. Now she navigated her lifeship well. Her mouth became a well of life to the people of Samaria.

Lois and Eunice raised Timothy in faith (2 Tim. 1:5; 3:14-15: Acts 16:1-5)

Lois, Timothy's grandmother, and Eunice, his mother, had a genuine faith in the Lord Jesus. They taught Timothy the way of salvation through the shed blood of Jesus Christ. He came to Christ at an early age.

These godly women taught him the basic truths of the Bible, to live for Jesus. He grew in the grace and knowledge of the Lord Jesus. No doubt, Timothy loved his father, a Greek, but he did not follow his ways.

One day the Apostle Paul came to Lystra and met Timothy. He was now a young man. He had a good testimony. News spread to Paul about him. "Go with me," Paul said. He saw in Timothy a good partner. He helped Paul establish the churches in the faith and win souls to Christ. He became like a son to Paul.

Lois and Eunice led young Timothy to Christ. The Lord used him to win many souls. He taught young churches how to lead people to the Lord. His mother and grandmother had a part in this. God says in Proverbs 11:18, "The wicked worketh a deceitful work: but to him that soweth righteousness shall be a sure reward." Lois and Eunice taught Timothy their faith. They shall surely reap a reward.

The Captain Calls

God gave us a responsibility, not only to steer away from the shoals ourselves, but also to help others avoid them. Our Captain tells us to go and share the gospel message. "Repent, repent," He says to the lost. When a woman repents, she turns from the paths of sin. She fears the Lord and trusts in Christ. She finds a fountain of life.

The Captain calls in Proverbs 13:14, "The law of the wise *is* a fountain of life, to depart from the snares of death." When you tell out the gospel and a woman repents, you rescue a soul from death.

The Captain cries, "If thou forbear to deliver *them that are* drawn unto death, and *those that are* ready to be slain; If thou sayest, Behold, we knew it not; doth not he that pondereth the heart consider *it*? and he that keepeth thy soul, doth *not* he know *it*? and shall *not* he render to *every* man according to his works?" (Prov. 24:11-12). Do we obey the command to go and share the gospel?

The Captain calls, "The lips of the righteous feed many: but fools die for want of wisdom" (Prov. 10:21). After a woman accepts the Saviour, do we encourage her to come for baptism? Explain to her what baptism means. Do we teach her to observe all things the Captain commanded? In this we disciple her. We train her in the Christian life. This feeds new converts.

"The fear of the Lord *is* a fountain of life, to depart from the snares of death" (Prov. 14:27), the Captain says. God promises a life-giving fountain to all who come to the Saviour. All who drink of it will depart from the snares of death.

The Captain cries, "The heart of the righteous studieth to answer: but the mouth of the wicked poureth out evil things" (Prov. 15:28). As we witness, people give excuses. They ask hard questions. This gives us an opportunity to study. Are we ready to give a reason of the hope within us? Do it with meekness, with fear, and with humility.

Challenges Today's Women Face

Are you wondering, *How can I begin?* First, introduce yourself and ask about their family, their work and hobbies. Then inquire about their religious background. "Did you used to go to church? Where?" Give a brief testimony and share the gospel with them.

How can we handle all the excuses they offer? How can we deal with their hard questions? Say, "That's a good question. We will get back to that later." Then continue with the gospel message. Some questions and excuses will not seem to matter after they receive Christ as their Saviour. If they come from a different background, some questions may still perplex them. If you do not know the answers, say, "I don't know. I 'll have to give that more study. I'll get back to you later."

Go home and search the Scriptures. Ask the pastor if you still do not understand. Some things we will not know this side of eternity. For example, we believe in the trinity, God is three persons, but we cannot explain it. Keep your promise if you said you would get back with them. Be honest with them.

You knock on a door, and a woman bursts out the door. She says, "What business do you have interrupting me? I'm busy getting dinner for my husband." What can we say? We may say, "I have something to tell you." Give the gospel message, and the woman may listen.

We greet a woman, "Good morning." They say, "What's good about it?" We may say, "I have good news for you." Then share the gospel with her.

We come to a widow's house. We may ask, "Do you ever think about having someone else come to live with you?" The widow says, "Oh, I'd give anything in the world if I could find someone to keep me company." We may say, "I know Somebody who will come and live with you." Then introduce the widow to Jesus Christ.

Make a roadmap in your Bible. Mark and number these verses in order: Romans 3:10; Romans 5:12; Romans 6:23; Romans 5:8; and Romans 10: 9, 10, 13. Now we can use our New Testament or small Bible to lead a soul to Christ.

Later, memorize these verses. Write them on cards. Carry them with us. Review them when we wait. If a woman will not allow us to read from the Bible, sometimes we can quote these verses to her.

Always carry gospel tracts with you. Leave them in restrooms; find other places to leave them. Think of creative ways to distribute them. Hand them out to clerks, customers, your doctor, dentist, and others. One car salesman puts one in the glove compartment of cars in his car lot.

"Follow Me," the Captain pleads. When we do, He makes us fishers of men. As we fish from our lifeship for souls, some come to Christ. Be persistent and keep fishing. An old song reads, "Never give up." Let us adopt this good motto.

Give the Helm to Jesus

If we want to win souls for Jesus, get ready for mocking and ridicule. People love their sin and its pleasures. As we seek to turn them from the coral reefs, do not expect smooth sailing. Be prepared and be persistent, but not overbearing. Be gentle and tactful with them. God promises, "Follow me, and I will make you fishers of men" (Matt. 4:19). Are we ready?

"Lay up heavenly treasures," the Captain calls to us. When we win souls and obey Him, we fill up our treasure chest in Heaven. God promises to reward us.

CHAPTER 11

Watch and Pray!

A godly woman prays often. God hears her prayers. Her Captain says, "Blessed *is* the man that heareth me, watching daily at my gates, waiting at the posts of my doors" (Prov. 8:34). She hears God's Word, watches at His gates, the place of authority, and waits on Him at the doorpost. God blesses her life.

Praying Sailors

The pirates call out to their god. If they cry for help to the true God, He does not hear them. Their sacrifices and prayers are an abomination to God—a hateful thing. Why? Because of their sin.

If we pray with sin in our hearts, God will not hear us. He hears humble sailors who confess and forsake their sins.

What is prayer? John R. Rice said that prayer is asking, seeking and knocking. O. Hallesby wrote a book entitled *Prayer* in 1931. He said, "To pray is to let Jesus into our hearts." When we pray in truth, we depend utterly upon God. The Captain moves us to pray.

God commands us to pray. The Captain promises to hear and answer the prayers of godly sailors. He says, "Call upon me, and I will show you great and mighty things which thou knowest not" (Jer. 33:3).

We pray because of who Jesus is and what He has done for us. This is what it means to pray "in Jesus' name". Tacking words onto the end of a prayer does not do it.

The Spirit of prayer, the Holy Spirit, lives in our hearts. He helps our weakness in prayer. We cannot hear Him audibly or the Lord Jesus as they intercede for us.

The Captain delights in the prayers of those who know Him. He says, "The effectual fervent prayer of a righteous man availeth much" (Jas. 5:16). An effectual, fervent prayer means a powerful prayer that comes from a burning heart. Prayer that availeth accomplishes its purpose. God hears and answers such prayers.

How can we pray like this? Pray in the Spirit, in faith, in a forgiving spirit, with all the heart, with a prepared and true heart, with confidence in God, with submission to God, with transparency, and with humility. In myself I cannot pray with even one of these characteristics. As I write this chapter, I learn and speak to myself. Only as God takes control of our lives can we pray effectively.

For what shall we pray? Ask for temporal blessing: food, clothing, shelter. Seek for spiritual blessing. Plead for mercy and grace when troubles bind us in them. Intercede for believers and for the lost.

The Captain implores us to avoid certain things in prayer: useless repetition and a showy exhibition, such as the Pharisees; discouragement; selfishness; sin; indifference; neglect of His Word; and doubt. One of the biggest sins is prayerlessness. God knows our needs, but He wants us to ask.

God delights to answer the prayers of His children. Get your heart right, pray from the heart, and God will hear and answer. Many times I feel so inadequate in my prayer life. However, God hears and answers my feeble prayers.

For example, My mother, legally blind, sat alone in her car when it started to roll. *The car is moving,* she said to herself. *I've got to do something.*

When we left the White Kitchen, a restaurant, the engine turned over, but neither of us could get it out of park.

What are we going to do? we thought. God is our hope, but we forgot to pray. Instead we used our human reasoning and it nearly spelled disaster.

I left Mom in the car, and used a pay phone. "Jack," I said, "My engine turns on, but I can't get it out of park."

"Is the wheel cramped tight against the curb?" he asked. "If it is, that can put the shift lever in a bind. Pull hard on it, and you may be able to shift it. Call me back and let me know if this works."

I found the wheel cramped tight against the curb. As Jack suggested, I yanked hard on the lever when the car started up. It worked, but I feared to put it back into park, I left the car running while I phoned Jack.

When I returned to the car, Mom's face had turned ashen white. She was shaking. "I almost had an accident," she said. "The car rolled all the way across the road. Two cars crossed behind me. My heart pounded as I expected to be plunged into eternity, but I heard no crash."

"I lunged across to the driver's seat. Gritting my teeth, I got the car into drive. I drove across the street and parked."

My heart palpitated. Mom, I thought, *cars don't drive themselves. Unseen hands grabbed the wheel and drove the car. Who parked the car back in the same spot as I had left it?* I saw the shift lever in park with the engine turned off.

Mom could have been killed, I thought. He still cares even though I forgot to pray.

God directed traffic that day and helped a blind woman to avert disaster. He protected Mom and me.[1]

Women Who Shipwrecked

Samson's wife—used by enemies (Jud. 14:1-17)

Samson saw a Philistine woman, an ungodly sailor. He begged his parents, "Go get her for me."

They rebuked him, "Isn't there a woman of our people to marry? Why do you go to these sinful Philistines?"

The men of the city held a marriage feast for this couple. Before this Samson saw a dead lion with honey bees swarming around it and honey in the carcass. At the feast he told a riddle, "Out of the eater came forth meat, and out of the strong came forth sweetness." No one came up with the solution.

The Philistines came to his wife, "Entice your husband, that he may tell the riddle."

She wept before Samson, and said, "You hate me; you do not love me. You did not tell me your riddle." Day after day she wept until Samson could take no more. He told it to her, and she told the Philistine men.

They came to Samson, "What is sweeter than honey?" they said. "What is stronger than a lion?"

These treacherous men threatened to burn his wife's house down if she failed to inform them. However, when Samson made them angry, they burnt her and her father with fire.

This woman could have asked Samson about the true God, but she did not. She worshipped the Philistine gods, though they did not move nor answer her prayers. God says in Proverbs 28:9, "He that turneth away his ear from hearing the law, even his prayer *shall* be abomination." She turned away her ear from God's Word. God hated her prayer.

Zebedee's wife asked unwisely (Matt. 20:20-23)

She came to Jesus with her sons, James and John, to ask a favor of Him. He said, "What do you desire?"

Zebedee's wife said, "Grant that these my two sons my sit, the one on your right hand, and the other on the left, in Thy kingdom." As many mothers, she entertained ambition for her sons.

Jesus answered, "You know not what you ask." He turned to her two sons, "Can you drink of the cup I will drink? Are you able to be baptized with my baptism?" He spoke of the cup of death, and the baptism of suffering.

"We are able," they answered.

The Lord said, "Ye shall drink of my cup. You will be baptized with the baptism that I am baptized with. However, you ask special privileges that I cannot give. Only my Father can do this."

God exalts the humble, those who serve others. The Captain hates the proud look (Prov. 6:16-17). He says, "Every one *that is* proud in heart is an abomination to the Lord: *though* hand *join* in hand, he shall not be unpunished" (Prov. 16:5). A proud woman asked a favor for her sons. The Captain did not honor her request.

Women Who Navigated Well

Hannah prayed about her troubles

Penninah provoked Hannah because she had children and Hannah had none. Jewish women considered this a terrible disgrace. They believed God punished them by making them barren.

Elkanah, Hannah's husband, dearly loved his wife, a devout woman. She fretted because she had no children. Her husband did not understand when she wept and refused to eat. He said, "Hannah, why do you weep? Why is your heart sad? Am I not better to you than ten children?"

Every year, her husband went up to Shiloh to worship the Lord. Hannah traveled with him. She went before the tabernacle and poured out her heart. She said, "O Lord, if Thou wilt look upon me and give me a man child, I will give him unto the Lord."

Eli, the priest, saw her lips move, but heard no voice. He concluded that she had over indulged. He said, "How long will you be drunk? Put away your wine."

Hannah said, "Sir, I am not drunk. I sorrow in my heart. I laid bare my soul before the Lord."

"Go in peace," Eli said. "God grant you your petition."

She left, ate, and sang songs in her heart. She knew the Lord would give her a son. God answered her prayer. She bore a child and called him Samuel, meaning "asked of God." After she weaned him, she brought him to Shiloh to serve the Lord. God blessed this woman. He gave her three more sons and two daughters (1 Sam. 1:6-10; 2:21).

Hannah trusted in the Lord as Proverbs 3:5-6 says. "Trust in the LORD with all thine heart; and lean not unto thine own understanding. In all thy ways acknowledge him, and he shall direct thy paths." God blessed Hannah for looking unto Him.

Anna, a devout woman (Luke 2:36-38)

Anna stayed around the temple. What did she do there? She fasted and prayed night and day. She lived a godly life-style.

Now this woman was an eighty-four-year old widow. She lived with her only husband for seven years. She knew no other man.

While Simeon blessed Mary, Joseph, and baby Jesus, Anna came to the temple area. She thanked the Lord and spoke to others of the Saviour. She talked to those who looked for their Redeemer, the One who came to pay the price for their sins.

This godly sailor belonged to the tribe of Asher. God called her a prophetess. In this office, she told the good news, "A Saviour has been born."

The Captain said, "The prayer of the upright *is* his delight" (Prov. 15:8). He delighted in Anna's prayers and fasting.

The Captain Calls

The Captain calls, "The LORD *is* far from the wicked: but he heareth the prayer of the righteous" (Prov. 15:29). The righteous have received Christ's righteousness by faith. Believer, God hears your prayers.

The Captain delights in your prayers as Proverbs 15:8 tells us. "The sacrifice of the wicked *is* an abomination to the LORD: but the prayer of the upright *is* his delight." The prayers of godly sailors makes Him happy.

However, if we harbor sin in our heart, the Lord will not hear us. The Captain says, in Proverbs 28:13, "He that covereth his sins shall not prosper: but whoso confesseth and forsaketh *them* shall have mercy." Confess sins and He cleanses us. Then we can live in victory.

The Captain says in Psalm 34:15, "The eyes of the LORD *are* upon the righteous, and his ears *are open* unto their cry." He listens to our prayers.

In Psalm 34:17 the Captain calls, "*The righteous* cry, and the LORD heareth, and delivereth them out of all their troubles." Sometimes, we have troubles. Call unto Him and find deliverance.

In Luke 18:1-8 the Captain speaks of a widow who came to an unjust judge. He did not fear God, nor regard man. This widow said, "Avenge me of my enemy." He kept putting her off, but she continued asking for help. Because he tired of her continual coming, he granted her request. God will hear and answer us when we cry day and night unto Him for relief. Be persistent in prayer.

The Captain tells a story in Luke 11:5-8 about a friend who had nothing to feed his guest. He came to a house at midnight, and said, "Friend, lend me three loaves for a friend of mine came to me and I have nothing to set before him." At first, his friend refused to get up and give him bread. However, his friend kept knocking at his door. He got up and gave him his request. When we ask God for something we need, let us persist as did this person. He answers prayer.

The Captain gave an illustration in Luke 18:9-14. He shows us that He does not listen to the proud, but hears the humble. He says in Psalm 9:12, "He forgetteth not the cry of the humble." No sailor is worthy of the least of God's mercies. Admit this in prayer. When we bow before the Almighty God. He will hear us.

"Blessed *is* the man that heareth me, watching daily at my gates, waiting at the posts of my doors" (Prov. 8:34).

Challenges Today's Women Face

Have you prayed for a loved one for many years? Do you feel God does not hear your prayers? Keep praying. My cousin called me a few years ago. She said, "I accepted Christ as my Saviour at camp when you talked with me." This occurred about forty-five years ago. One lady said, "I prayed for my husband for twenty years." He came to Christ about two years ago. His life shows evidence of growth. My Mom accepted Christ in the final year of her ninety-seven years, about 48 years after my conversion. God hears and answers prayer.

What do you need? I needed a piano to teach piano lessons. One day the pastor called and said he had something to show me. When I met him at the church, he led me into a classroom and asked, "Would this piano do?" I called the piano tuner. He tuned it good enough for my lessons. I enjoyed playing it myself. Pray for your needs. The Lord gives pianos and other things where a genuine need exists.

What do you desire? Do you have a longing in your heart for something? One barren couple wanted a child. They prayed, "Lord, give us a child we can adopt," but they failed to specify how many. The adoption agency offered them twins. They smiled and took them home. Pray for your deepest longings; the Lord delights to answer prayers.

What do you need the Lord to stop or send? One time Rose and I visited in a housing project. Children kept coming and coming to hear about Jesus. Time passed quickly. Suppertime came. We did not want to keep our hostess waiting. One child said, "Can I go get my twin?" We promised to come back tomorrow. The next day the rain poured down in torrents. "Lord, please stop the rain so that we can go back to the housing project," we prayed. About 2:00 p.m. the rain stopped. We visited the housing project again. God can stop or send rain or other things in answer to prayer. Pray earnestly; God answers prayer.[2]

Give the Helm to Jesus

Plead and cry unto the Lord. He can do great and mighty things. "Call unto me, and I will answer thee, and shew thee great and mighty things, which thou knowest not" (Jer. 33:3). He does not look for those in high places, only a humble believer. He delights in our prayers.

God gave the believer the wondrous privilege of prayer. He loves to hear His children pray.

Endnotes

1 "A Blind Woman Drives," by Lynn Wallace. The Spiritual Voice News, Spring 2005, page 7.

2 "Please Stop the Rain" by Lynn Wallace in *Conquest* (now *Horizons*), Vol. 31, Issue 3, pages 1-2, 4. Regular Baptist Press, Schaumburg IL, Spring Quarter, 1998.

CHAPTER 12

Watch and Obey!

The godly sailor gladly receives the Captain's commandments and endeavors to keep them. His Word says, "The wise in heart will receive commandments: but a prating fool shall fall" (Prov. 10:8). A wise woman regards His words. She does not speak with prating words [idle talk], but with those profitable unto others.

Obedient Sailors

The prating fool will fall. She talks on and on about nothing that matters. The Captain advises us to watch our lips. Most of us like to talk. The godly sailor has learned to listen and to minister to the needs of others. She obeys God's Word, curbs her lips, and avoids a multitude of words.

This godly woman fears God's commands. She loves His Word and listens to Him. The Captain will reward her. She listens to God. He hides her from the pirates in His pavillion where she feels safe and does not fear evil.

A godly sailor trusts in God's mercy and truth in her heart. The Captain blesses her and gives her understanding. Because she shows tact in her dealings with others, she finds favor in their sight.

The keeping of God's commands brings health, enjoyment of life, and peace in her heart. This godly woman gives the Captain her heart and observes His ways from her Logbook. She rejoices in serving Him and seeking to bring others to her Lord.

The Captain does great things in answer to the prayers of those who seek to obey Him. He can stop the rain or send rain. He can bless a childless couple with a baby or babies. He can give a piano to one seeking to teach piano. He can bring an elderly parent to Himself. Our Captain does mighty things when we pray.

For example, I prayed for four long years, "Lord, what wilt Thou have me to do?" The heavens remained silent. I taught primaries in Sunday School, typed letters for my pastor, played the piano, and taught children's Bible classes. However, somewhere I had lost my joy. I thought, *God has put me on the shelf; I'll have to do the best I can.*

Why did I wait so long? Perhaps to teach me patience or because I did not fully trust the Lord. The Lord may have waited to perfect His work in a man—the one He later led me to marry.

After three years of waiting, Ron Corley, a missionary to the Navajo Indian, preached in my church. He probably noticed my downcast look when busy serving the Lord. He said, "Why not come down to the Navajo?" I said, "God did not call me to the Navajo." This did not convince him. He prayed for me.

The next year Ron returned to Montrose, Colorado where I lived. He said, "Lynn, why don't you come down and visit us for a week or two?" I agreed to go. *I will have a nice vacation,* I thought.

God had different plans. One day we went to the backside of the reservation. We arrived early and made some visits. One woman said, "*Yáʼátʼééh*" to me. I repeated the greeting to her.

Later, when I asked the missionary, "Does *yáʼátʼééh* mean "hello"? He said, "You're a pretty good Navajo." Only one word, but God used it to break down an excuse. In my heart I said, *I can never learn Navajo.*

One night I slipped to the guest room with my Bible. Words from Isaiah 42:6-7 leaped off the page at me. "I the Lord have called thee in righteousness,…To open the blind eyes, to bring out the prisoners from the prison, and them that sit in darkness out of the prison house."

No longer could I argue, "I'm not called to the Navajo." These Indians were blinded to the truth. They languished in the prison house of sin. They sat in darkness.

To the Navajo I went. About a year later, a man named Leon Wallace came to work with the Corley's. He asked me to marry him. The Lord led us together and gave us a child. We served on the Navajo mission field. Our baby opened doors for us.

Sixteen years later, He called my husband home to glory. He said, "Lynn, I want you to write for me." Since then, I wrote many things. God blessed me with rejection slips and publication. He answered my prayer, "Lord, what wilt Thou have me to do."

Women Who Shipwrecked

Zipporah, Moses' Wife—shunned God's command (Exo. 2:16-22; 4:24-26; 18:1-4)

Zipporah met Moses when she and her six sisters came to the well to draw water. Moses helped these seven women get their water from the well.

Zipporah's father, Jethro, was the priest of Midian. Jethro gave his daughter, Zipporah, to Moses for his wife. She bore two sons, Gershom and Eliezer.

The Jewish law, given by God, required every male child to be circumcised. Zipporah disliked the task that fell to her. She called Moses "a bloody husband." She obeyed, but not cheerfully.

Moses' wife kept the letter of the law, but her attitude was wrong. God intended this rite to picture a changed heart and putting away sin. God says, "Give me thine heart, and let thine eyes observe my ways" (Prov. 23:26). Zipporah did not receive the blessing of obedience because she shunned God's command.

Women Idolaters—turned away from God (Jer. 7:18; 44:15-25; Eze. 8:13-14)

These women kneaded dough to make cakes to the queen of heaven. They said, "We will do whatever comes out of our mouth." They made vows to burn incense unto the moon and to pour out drink offerings unto her. They broke their vows to God, but refused to break these idolatrous vows. They burned their moon-shaped cakes to her honor. They made false claims that this goddess supplied all their needs and protected them.

They said, "Since we quit pouring out our drink offerings to her, we have wanted all things. The sword and the famine have devoured us." They deceived themselves. God provided for them and protected them. In His longsuffering, He suffered with them, giving them time to repent. However, they refused. Then the Captain withheld His blessings from them and punished them—a punishment justly deserved because they turned their backs to Him.

Their words, "We will not hearken unto Thee," condemned them to servitude in Babylon." Some died in Egypt because they ignored God's words when He forbid them to go there.

In Ezekiel 8:13-14 God showed the women weeping for Tammuz, an idol. They wept for the sorrows of this impure god—an imagination of the human heart. They chose to worship this false god rather than worship and serve the true and living God. The pagan people observed lewd rites in this carnal worship, and these reprobate Jews joined them.

Their turning away from God—their disobedience—filled them with the fruit of their own evil hearts. "For the turning away of the simple shall slay them, and the prosperity of fools shall destroy them" (Prov. 1:32). Their own foolishness in following idols destroyed them.

Women Who Navigated Well

Women Spinners—worked willingly (Exo. 35:4-26)

Women spun cloth for the tabernacle—a tent for meeting with God in the wilderness. God commanded the people to make all that this place needed. These women had willing hearts to do this for their Lord. They made blue, purple, scarlet and fine linen yard goods.

Some made a hanging for the court gate and for the court. Other women made clothes for Aaron, the high priest, and his sons. Skillfully, women wove the cloth for the veil—the curtain between the holy of holies and the holy place. They embroidered it according to the Captain's pattern. Willing hands spun the hanging for the door of the tabernacle.

Because of these willing women helpers, the tent appeared beautiful on the inside, plain on the outside. All who come to Christ can see His beauty, but it is hidden to those who reject Him.

The Captain blessed the sailors who spun cloth for the tabernacle. He says, "For the commandment is a lamp; and the law is light; and reproofs of instruction are the way of life" (Prov. 6:23). His command became a lamp to these obedient women.

Priscilla—suffered for Christ (Acts 18:2-26; Rom. 16:3-5)
Priscilla with her husband, Aquilla, made tents. The apostle Paul, a tentmaker, stayed with them because they employed themselves in the same craft. They lived in Corinth and helped Paul in the ministry.

When Paul departed for Syria, he took Priscilla and Aquilla with him. He left them in Ephesus while he traveled on to Jerusalem. While there, they met Apollos who knew only part of the Word of God. Priscilla and Aquilla heard him preach in the synagogue. They explained the Word of God to him that he had not heard.

Priscilla and Aquilla risked their lives for Paul's sake. He thanked the Captain for them and commended them to the church at Rome.

Priscilla kept the ways of God. God said in Proverbs 8:32, "Now therefore hearken unto me, O ye children: for blessed *are they that* keep my ways." Because Priscilla obeyed God, He blessed her.

The Captain Calls
The Captain calls, "Now therefore hearken unto me, O ye children: for blessed are they that keep my ways" (Prov. 8:32). God blesses godly women who keep His Word. An obedient sailor loves the Word and delights in His ways.

A godly sailor remembers her Captain's commandment, "Be not rash with thy mouth;…let thy words be few" (Eccl. 5:2). If her friend reproves her, she takes it in a meek spirit. As the Captain says, "As an earring of gold, and an ornament of fine gold, *so is* a wise reprover upon an obedient ear" (Prov. 25:12). She humbly bows before the truth, and seeks to learn by it.

She hearkens to the counsel she finds in God's Word. The Captain cries, "The way of a fool *is* right in his own eyes: but he that hearkeneth unto counsel *is* wise" (Prov. 12:15). She is not conceited, but she knows God's way is best.

"Seek ye first the kingdom of God, and his righteousness;" our Captain says, "and all these things shall be added unto you" (Matt. 6:33). In previous verses, He talked about things we need for this life, such as food and clothing. When we put God first, He will take care of all our material needs.

The Christian life is a narrow way, but as we walk in this path, God blesses us along the way. He sometimes surprises us with things for which we did not even ask. "Walk as children of light," the Captain calls to us (Eph. 5:8). "God is light".(1 John 1:5). He has given us His righteousness and His light. When we walk in the light, we will not stumble, as those who walk in darkness [sin]. He wants us to walk as Christ walked (1 John 2:6).

However, all sailors have that old sin nature. What can we do? Confess it. God will cleanse us and forgive us (1 John 1:9). Then get up and walk in victory.

Many false prophets [tellers of lies] are in the world today. The Captain says, "Beware of false prophets, which come to you in sheep's clothing, but inwardly they are ravening wolves" (Matt. 7:15). Satan himself appears as an "angel of light." His ministers transform themselves as "ministers of righteousness" (2 Cor. 11:14-15).

What can we do? How can we recognize them? The Captain calls, "Hear instruction, and be wise, and refuse it not" (Prov. 8:33). Know your Bible. If they do not speak according to the words of this Book, they are of their father the devil, the father of lies (John 8:44). Do not listen to them. Reprove them.

The Captain cries, "He *is in* the way of life that keepeth instruction: but he that refuseth reproof erreth" (Prov. 10:17). Do they believe Jesus Christ is God in the flesh? (John 1:1, 14). Do they believe salvation from sin is in Him and Him alone? (Acts 4:12; John 14:6). Try the spirits and see if they be of God (1 John 4:1). Do not be afraid for "Greater is He that is in you than he that is in the world" (1 John 4:4). God defeated Satan at the cross. We can have victory. Trust in the Lord.

"Let not mercy and truth forsake thee: bind them about thy neck; write them upon the table of thine heart: So shalt thou find favour and good understanding in the sight of God and man" (Prov. 3:3-4).

Challenges Today's Women Face

God commands us to "love one another." Do you love that unruly child who disrupts your Sunday School class? A young boy walked around when he pleased. Nobody taught him to sit still. The people in our church showed love to him. His mother came to pick him up from Daily Vacation Bible School. A worker led her to the Lord. Both parents came the following Sunday. At the close of the service, the father accepted the Lord. Love those difficult children. You may see great results.

We may have "good" kids, but none of us has perfect kids. Discipline makes them accountable when they do wrong. Afterwards, show them you love them. Praise encourages them when they do right. These two elements cause them to want to obey. Be consistent.

The Saviour directs us, "Walk the narrow way." When we come to Christ, we turn on this path. However, temptations come to veer us this way or that. The Captain does not promise us an easy road, but a blessed one. When we stay on the right path, He will bless us. We will find pleasures of which we never dreamed.

The Captain pleads, "Seek the kingdom of God and His righteousness." Then He promises to take care of our basic needs. Sometimes, He even grants our fondest dreams. We all have our priorities. Ask a teenager what she wants. Some will answer, "I want to get married and raise a family." Others dream of making lots of money or being famous. How many of us put God first in our lives? God desires the best for us, but we hinder Him when we let other things get in our way.

Give the Helm to Jesus

God is light and provides a light for our path. He says, "For the commandment *is* a lamp; and the law *is* light; and reproofs of instruction *are* the way of life" (Prov. 6:23). Let us walk in His light and seek to obey His commands. This is the path of blessing.

The Lord's commands do not make it hard for us. His yoke is easy and His burden light. Follow His way and He gives us peace and rest.

CHAPTER 13

Watch That Temper!

A temper out of control upsets our lifeship. The Captain says, "*He that is* slow to wrath *is* of great understanding: but *he that is* hasty of spirit exalteth folly" (Prov. 14:29). Do not lose it! Be prudent. If your husband utters a bad word, do not shout, "Don't you say that to me." Instead, say softly, "Honey, do you know what you just said? That kind of words dishonors our God."

Prudent Sailors

Understanding keeps the godly sailor from troubles. It helps her get along with others. She loves her family, and does not talk about her children's foibles. She and her husband deal with them privately.

She plans ahead of time, and does not believe everything she hears. If someone starts to gossip or tell a dirty joke, she suppresses it. About gossip, she may say, "Let's go ask the person about whom you're talking." This will stop it quickly. She refuses to listen to dirty jokes and quietly walks away. Soon the crowd will say, "Here comes that 'preacher'. We can't talk about that around her." If they tease you, ignore it. You take away their fun when it does not annoy you.

A discreet and prudent sailor discerns between right and wrong. She seeks to do right. Carefully, she weighs both sides of the issue before she makes a decision.

If someone offends her, she prays about it first. Then she goes privately to that sailor to try to make things right. Only when her Christian sister is obstinate will she take two or three with her.

Extreme cases go before the church. We can resolve most conflicts if we go with the right attitude when offended.

Discretion defers anger. A godly sailor forgives quickly. If she offends someone, she does not glibly say, "I'm sorry," but she genuinely apologizes, and does whatever she can to make it right. She humbly admits it when she is wrong.

For example, one time when we lived in Dallas, Texas, I forgot my husband's uniforms. We went back to the laundomat but we did not find them. On the way home, I vented my temper on myself.

A prudent women keeps silent in such cases. My explosion thundered as fury poured on Leon, my husband, and Lynette, my daughter. Words like, "I'm sorry I forgot your uniforms," bring a calm on life's turbulent seas. God says, "Be ye angry and sin not" (Eph. 4:26). I not only forgot Leon's uniforms, but God's Word as well.

After I confessed my sin, God graciously forgave me and gave me the victory.

Women Who Shipwrecked

Peninnah, Elkanah's wife—Provoked Hannah (1 Sam. 1:1-6)

When Elkanah gave a larger portion to Hannah, his wife, it aggravated Peninnah, his other wife. She bore him several children. To retaliate she provoked Hannah who had no children.

Perhaps Peninnah felt her husband used her, and did not love her. Every year at a certain time, he gave Hannah a larger and better gift. He gave her a "worthy portion," and to his other wife and his children shares.

When Hannah went up to the house of the Lord, her adversary provoked her sore. She wept and lost her appetite.

This created a miserable situation for both Elkanah's wives. God never condoned bigamy. It leads to jealousy, anger, and hatred. It forced Peninnah and Hannah to share a husband and brought about an unhappy home. As God says, "Jealousy *is* the rage of a man" (Prov. 6:34). Every year Hannah received a better part than Peninnah. This induced jealous rage in this home.

Michal—scoffed at David (1 Sam. 18:20-28; 2 Sam. 6:12-23)

King Saul promised to give his daughter, Michal, to David for his wife. He did this to ensnare him. He did not ask for a dowry of money, but for David to bring proof that he killed one hundred Philistines. He thought to make David fall into the hands of his enemies. Saul hated David and wanted him dead.

However, the king's request pleased David, a man of war. He slew two hundred Philistines, and brought back twice what King Saul requested. Michal loved David and the Lord went with him. The ruler trembled before him.

Michal protected David when Saul sought to kill him. She said, "If you don't save your life tonight, tomorrow you'll be slain." She put an image in his bed to fool the king, and let David down through a window. He fled and escaped.

However, when David brought the ark to Jerusalem and danced for joy, it displeased Michal. Before she loved and protected him, but now she despised him. Her temper flared.

She falsely accused David of vanity. He answered her that he danced before the Lord. God judged Michal. She bore David no children—a terrible disgrace to a Jewess. Proverbs 21:23 says, "Whoso keepeth his mouth and his tongue keepeth his soul from troubles." Michal opened her mouth instead of keeping silent. Because she spoke unwisely, she had troubles.

Women Who Navigated Well

Mary of Bethany—Honored Jesus (Luke 39:39-42; 13:1-8)

When Jesus went to Jerusalem, He went often to the house of Mary and Martha who lived in Bethany (about fifteen miles from Jerusalem).

Mary sat at Jesus' feet. She loved to hear Him talk and teach her about God. She did not have a complete Bible as we do, but only the Old Testament. She learned much when she lingered around her Lord.

This irritated Martha, her sister, who wanted everything in place for this special guest. She spent time preparing a sumptuous meal.

"Lord," she said, "Dost Thou not care that my sister has left me alone to serve Thee? Bid her come and help me."

Jesus answered, "Martha, Martha, you worry about many things. Mary chose that good part. No one shall take it away from her."

After this, six days before the Passover Feast, Jesus visited Mary, and Martha. Their brother, Lazarus, whom Jesus had raised from the dead, enjoyed the visit, too. The two sisters cooked a meal for Jesus. Martha served this delicious meal.

Mary broke a box of expensive perfume. She poured it over the head and feet of her Master. Some criticized her and said, "She could have sold it and gave the money to the poor." Mary could have bought costly garments for herself, but she cared for her Saviour and did this for Him.

Jesus said, "She kept the ointment for my burial, Wherever people preach the gospel, they will speak of this as a memorial for her."

Mary had the right attitude. Her actions pricked some. They cared not about the poor, but coveted for themselves. The Captain said in Proverbs 12:8, "A man shall be commended according to his wisdom: but he that is of a perverse heart shall be despised." Those who criticized Mary had wayward hearts. Jesus commended Mary for her wisdom, foresight, and her outpouring of love toward Him.

A Greek Woman—accepted criticism (Matt. 15:21-28; Mark 7:24-30)

This Grecian woman lived in Phoenicia, near the towns of Tyre and Sidon. The Bible also calls her "a woman of Canaan."

Jesus approached her hometown. He entered a house to hide from the crowds. However, this woman heard of Him. She came and fell down at His feet. She worshipped Him.

"Have mercy on me, O Lord, Thou Son of David," this Canaanite called out, "My daughter is grievously vexed with a devil."

When Jesus gave her no answer, this foreigner kept silent. His disciples said, "Send her away. She troubles us."

Jesus said, "I am not sent, but to the lost sheep of the house of Israel."

Still at His feet, she bowed her head, and cried out, "Lord, help me."

"It is not meet [fit] to take the children's bread, and cast it to dogs," He said.

This woman did not give up or explode because Jesus called her a dog. Jews called the Gentiles [non-Jews] this. She said, "Truth, Lord, yet the dogs eat the crumbs which fall from the master's table." She believed these crumbs from the Master's table could heal her daughter.

Jesus answered her, "O woman, great is thy faith. Go your way. The devil is gone out of your daughter."

The woman skipped home, found her daughter well. The Captain says, "*He that is* slow to wrath is of great understanding: but *he that is* hasty of spirit exalteth folly" (Prov. 14:29). Though an alien from the house of Israel, she believed the Master, and had great understanding.

The Captain Calls

The Captain calls, "Discretion shall preserve thee, understanding shall keep thee" (Prov. 2:11). When we understand knowledge, avoid wrong paths, and choose the right paths, it will keep us from the evil man and woman. God will give us wisdom.

"A fool's wrath is presently known," the Captain says in Proverbs 12:16, "but a prudent *man* covereth shame." The prudent sailor does not air all her flaws. She confesses them in private prayer. If she sinned against another person, she confesses her faults to that one, and asks for forgiveness.

The Captain calls, "A soft answer turneth away wrath: but grievous words stir up anger" (Prov. 15:1). If her Christian sister spouts out angry words, a godly sailor prays silently for wisdom. Then she answers with soft words. Usually, this turns away anger.

The Jews won many victories over cities, and God directed them in this. The Canaanites committed wicked things. In their worship of idols, they prostituted themselves, and cast their babies into a fiery furnace. God blessed His people in giving them victory over a people with these vile practices. However, the Captain says, "*He that is* slow to anger *is* better than the mighty; and he that ruleth his spirit than he that taketh a city" (Prov. 16:32).

The Captain cries, "Make no friendship with an angry man; and with a furious man thou shalt not go: Lest thou learn his ways, and get a snare to thy soul" (Prov. 22:24-25). Stay away from angry sailors. They often make tempers flare and get people into trouble.

Do you have hard decisions to make? The Captain says, "Ask God for wisdom. He promises to give it" (Prov. 2:6; Jas. 1:5). If you have a godly husband, ask him. In hard cases go to your pastor. Trust in the Lord. A prudent woman does not make quick decisions. She speaks with sweet words. This increases the learning of others.

"A prudent *man* foreseeth the evil, *and* hideth himself; *but* the simple pass on, *and* are punished," says the Captain in Proverbs 27:12. In evil times a prudent woman keeps silent (Amos 5:13). She warns her children to stay away from strangers.

"The simple believeth every word: but the prudent *man* looketh well to his going. A wise *man* feareth, and departeth from evil: but the fool rageth, and is confident" (Prov. 14:15-16).

Challenges Today's Women Face

What can a woman do who has trouble with her temper? She can pray about it, ask for God's help and victory in this area. A short walk gives her time to cool off. Do you have small children? Engage them in quiet activities and pray. One poor woman had many children in a small house. When they saw her with an apron over her head, they knew she was praying. They played quietly.

What makes you angry? Does an obstinate child frustrate you? Walk a little ways away and pray for him. Try to find some way to show love for this child. Cook a special meal or fix his favorite dessert. He may say, "I'm not hungry." Then he comes back later and devours it. Your thoughtfulness may cause your child to feel ashamed. Sometimes, he apologizes.

A child stays angry. He resents his stepdad. Ask the child, "Why are you so angry?" Explain the situation to him. Try to help him understand. If his Dad is still alive, do not talk against him to the children. Be honest with them.

Broken promises can make a child angry. Do not promise a child anything. You may say, "If the weather stays nice and something else doesn't come up, we will try to go to the park" or whatever you plan. If he does not listen, or misunderstands you, he may say, "You said we were going to the park." Get his attention and make sure his eyes focus on you. Perhaps, it works better on a nice day to surprise your child and take him to the park.

Try to keep things in control to prevent angry children. Be as patient as possible with them. Explain the rules to them so that they understand.

What can we do when a woman takes something we said in the wrong way? She vents her anger. Be pleasant. If we said the wrong thing, apologize. We can say, "I'm sorry." Do our actions and facial expressions show it? Go home and pray for them everyday. Be kind. Take over cookies or flowers. Watch our words. Pray, "Lord, keep the door of my lips."

Sometimes, we make a mistake or sin. We vent our anger on ourselves. What can we do? Do not have a pity party. Learn from mistakes. If you sinned, confess them to God. Someone else gets hurt. Apologize and try to make things right. Try to make peace with them.

The husband comes home grumpy and tired. What can you do? Be sweet and kind. Fix a special meal for him. Keep silent about his ill temper. A good temper and a hot meal may help his bad mood. If he had a bad day at work, be sympathetic, and a good listener if he needs to talk.

Give the Helm to Jesus

Nearly every woman loses her temper at times. We cannot tame this beast ourselves, but God can bring it under control. He says, "The discretion of a man (or woman) deferreth his anger; and *it is* his glory to pass over a transgression" (Prov. 19:11).

Place anger in God's hands, and let Him help with the problem. He gives the victory.

Endnotes

1 "In God's Pavillion," by Lynn Wallace. Prayer Support for Women (online), October 30, 2005.

CHAPTER 14

Watch That Character

A woman of integrity sets her face like a flint. She maintains a godly character. As she sails on life's seas, she does not bend to every whim. "The integrity of the upright shall guide them: but the perverseness of transgressors shall destroy them" (Prov. 11:3). Her ship will land safely on the shore.

Women of Integrity

What is integrity? A woman of integrity lives a truthful and honest life. Not a hypocrite, she shows sincerity in her life-style and her convictions. She walks in moral uprightness. God looks on her heart and sees a woman of a godly character. Righteousness characterizes her life.

The ungodly may try to smear her reputation, but her character they cannot touch. Your reputation refers to what men think you are; character speaks of what you are. This does not mean sinless perfection, for all have a sinful nature inherited from Adam.

As this sailor seeks to follow God's way, He strengthens her and gives her boldness to stand up for the right. He directs her paths day by day. As bad sailors threaten her, the Captain delivers her out of trouble.

Few women of integrity possess much of this world's goods, yet they remain content with the heavenly treasures they lay up above.

On the other hand, the Captain calls ungodly sailors an abomination. This means He hates their deeds, not their souls. God loves them and wants them to repent of their wicked deeds and come to Him (John 3:16; 2 Pet. 3:9).

The deeds of the ungodly cause them to fall by their own wickedness. Sin destroys the sinners who refuse to repent. The Captain considers even their sacrifices an abomination because they refuse to turn their hearts toward Him.

The Lord delights in those who hold fast to their integrity. It pleases Him when sailors refuse to compromise with the world. These women hold their standards high, yet gentleness and kindness prevails in their lives. God blesses their lifeship.

Where does she obtain her inner strength? Daily, she communes with her Captain and pours over His Logbook. This precious book guides her as she sails on life's sea.

God gives her an understanding of the Bible and toward all who sail on life's seas. This godly sailor pleases God because she treats others right. Because of her consideration for wayward sailors, she draws them to her Lord.

For example, Ellen Oehms lay for months with pain. In the midst of all her suffering, she showed concern for others, and asked about people in her church.

In these long pain-filled hours at night she turned her thoughts to the Lord. When at last she could attend church again, she testified, "I'm thankful when pains keep me awake at night. On such occasions I have more time to pray."

Later, she resided in a nursing home, debilitated and in a wheelchair. "How are you?" she asked the residents, wheeling toward them. "Jesus is with you." She refreshes even the visitors.

Ellen was human like the rest of us. How could she think of others when her own needs were so great? She said, "I have known the Lord about fifty years, and I still have much to learn. I place my full dependence on Him."

This woman of integrity rejoiced because she placed her faith in the Lord, not in her circumstances. She readily admitted she had shortcomings, but reached out to others and relied on the Lord.[1] Now she has gone to Heaven to reap her eternal rewards.

Women Who Shipwrecked

Bathsheba—defiled (2 Sam. 11-12)

In those days people lacked modern plumbing. Number three tubs did not exist then. [Much later people used them who had no bathrooms.] Bible people often bathed outside. Some used streams.

Bathsheba bathed outside, perhaps in her garden. David looked down from his flat roof and saw this beautiful woman. He wanted her and sent for her. He took her, went unto her and lay with her.

David, the king, belonged at war to lead his army. Nonetheless, he stayed home. He defiled Bathsheba. David and she committed the scarlet sin. Uriah, an army captain and her husband, went to war.

Did Bathsheba fear David because he was the king? Perhaps. However, her integrity mattered more in God's sight. If she refused to go, when David sent for her, it may anger him. On the other hand, it may convict David of his sin. He knew he did wrong.

Bathsheba sent word to David that she carried his child in her body. David and she faced the death penalty for their adultery. David tried to get Uriah to go home. Then people would assume the baby belonged to Uriah. He refused and slept that night on David's doorstep. He said, "The captain and his army are encamped in the open fields. Should I go into mine house? I will not."

A desperate man, David sent a letter to Joab, his army captain. It said, "Set ye Uriah in the forefront of the hottest battle…that he may be smitten and die." Joab did so. The enemy killed Uriah in battle. David added murder to his sin of adultery.

Bathsheba bore an illegitimate son. She mourned when she heard her husband lost his life in the war. After mourning for her husband, she married David. She wept when the son of their unlawful union died. God blessed her and David with another son, Solomon. She lived to see him crowned king.

The Lord forgave both David and Bathsheba. However, they suffered much heartache because of their sin. God said, "Enter not into the path of the wicked, and go not in the way of evil *men*" (Prov. 4:14). Bathsheba, no doubt, wished that she fled from David when he sent for her.

Solomon's Outlandish Women—caused him to sin (1 Kin. 11:1-13)

King Solomon married many foreign women. God said of this, "Did not Solomon king of Israel sin by these things? yet among many nations was there no king like him, who was beloved of his God, and God made him king over all Israel: nevertheless even him did outlandish women cause to sin" (Neh. 13:26).

They enticed Solomon to worship their gods. He bowed before Ashtoreth, the goddess of the Zidonians. The king served Milcom, the god of the Ammonites. He built a high place for Chemosh, the Moabite god. This man constructed an altar for Molech, another Ammonite god. Solomon did the same for all these outlandish women.

Prostitution constituted a part of the worship of these false gods. The Captain said the Gentiles sacrificed to devils in their rituals (1 Cor. 10:20).

None of these foreigners inquired after the true God, though Solomon built the temple of God. They caused King Solomon to lose his testimony. Perhaps, he thought of this when he exhorted his son, Rehoboam. "Do not go after ungodly women." We find these warnings repeatedly in the book of Proverbs (chapters 5, 6, 7, 9, and other places). No doubt, Solomon wished he kept his heart pure and married the woman of Proverbs 31.

Women Who Navigated Well

Huldah—Prophetess (2 Chr. 34:14-28)

Huldah prophesied in the days of Josiah. She lived in Jerusalem. The Jews say that she was a prophetess among the women, the court ladies.

They found the book of the law in the temple when they repaired it. Shaphan the scribe said to King Josiah, "The priest hath given me a book." Josiah read this book before the king. He tore his clothes and wept. He said, "Go inquire of the LORD for me."

Shaphan, the priest and officers went to Huldah, the prophetess. She said, "Tell the man who sent you to me, thus saith the LORD, I will bring evil upon this place . . . Because they have forsaken me, my wrath shall be poured upon this place. It shall not be quenched."

However, Huldah said, "Say ye to the king, Thine heart was tender. Thou didst humble thyself before God. Thou didst rend thy clothes, and weep before God. Because of this, thou shalt be gathered to thy fathers in peace. Thine eyes shall not see all the evil I will bring upon this place." They sent word to the king.

Huldah, a wife in Israel, faithfully proclaimed God's word to the king. God said in Proverbs 25:13, "As the cold of snow in the time of harvest, *so is* a faithful messenger to them that send him: for he refresheth the soul of his masters." This woman of integrity refreshed the heart of the king.

The Virtuous Woman—faithful (Prov. 31:10-31)

The virtuous woman is worth more than rubies or diamonds. Her husband trusts her. She becomes a crown to him and remains faithful to him for life. She honors him and treats him right.

She works willingly with her hands. She buys yard goods and makes clothes for herself and her family. Her family dresses in warm clothing in the winter. They enjoy her tasty dishes, with spices from the orient.

Every morning, she rises early to prepare a nourishing breakfast for her family. The aroma of delicious stew permeates the house.

She buys a field and plants all kinds of vegetables. In another plot she plants fruit trees and grape vines.

In the evenings she spends time with her family. Her husband reads the Bible and explains it while she listens attentively. When she tucks her children into bed, she prays with them.

Her hands make good things to sell and share with the poor.

She speaks with wisdom and kindness. Her children respect her. Her husband praises her. She makes herself attractive to her husband, but her real beauty lies within her heart. She fears the Lord. People praise her for her good works. God says in Proverbs 20:7 "The just *man* walketh in his integrity: his children *are* blessed after him." This woman delights her husband.

The Captain Calls

"Let not mercy and truth forsake thee," the Captain calls. "Bind them about thy neck. Write them upon the table of thine heart" (Prov. 3:3). Mercy and truth accompany the woman of integrity.

The Captain says, "Let thine eyes look right on, and let thine eyelids look straight before thee....Turn not to the right hand nor to the left: remove thy foot from evil" (Prov. 4:25, 27). The godly woman turns from sin to follow her Captain.

"The way of the Lord *is* strength to the upright," the Captain assures us. However, He warns, "Destruction *shall be* to the workers of iniquity" (Prov. 10:29). A woman of a good character guides her lifeship in His paths.

The Captain cries out, "The righteousness of the perfect shall direct his way: but the wicked shall fall by his own wickedness" (Prov. 11:5). Any righteousness a woman has, she received from the Lord. His righteousness directs her. Perfect here means integrity. Only a believer in Jesus Christ has this.

"The righteousness of the upright shall deliver them: but transgressors shall be taken in *their own* naughtiness," the Captain says (Prov. 11:6). Her righteousness from the Lord not only directs this sailor, but delivers her when she has trials and temptations.

The Captain warns the ungodly and comforts us, "They that are of a froward heart *are* abomination to the Lord: but *such as are* upright in *their* way are his delight" (Prov. 11:20). He offers further warning and consolation, "The house of the wicked shall be overthrown: but the tabernacle of the upright shall flourish" (Prov. 14:11).

He delights in our prayers. The Captain says, "The prayer of the upright *is* his delight." However, "The sacrifice of the wicked *is* an abomination to the Lord" (Prov. 15:8).

"The highway of the upright *is* to depart from evil," the Captain calls. "He that keepeth his way preserveth his soul" (Prov. 16:17). The Lord is the One that keeps us. The good sailor preserves herself from falling by trusting in God and taking a stand against evil.

"The integrity of the upright shall guide them: but the perverseness of transgressors shall destroy them" (Prov. 11:3).

Challenges Today's Women Face

What do we do when everything seems to go wrong? Somebody ran into our cars and totaled it. The screen door stops working in the heat of summer. We hear distressing news from our child. People reproach us for our faith. Our house is falling apart. Two windows break and let in the bitter cold of winter. Our door lock breaks. Vandals come in and trash our house. We hope that all of these things do not happen at once, but often troubles seem to come in three's.

Do we pray and ask God, "Whom shall I call?" Do we have friends who help us clean up the mess the vandals made? Do we smile and say, "Bible Thumpers is not such a bad name?" Do we call our child and try to cheer him up? Why do such things happen? We may never know the answer this side of eternity. Perhaps our troubles can give us more compassion and understanding towards others.

What can we do if we suffer from health problems? We do not feel like doing what we want to do. Pray about it and ask the Lord for help. He can heal, but this may not be His will. Sometimes, we have to learn to accept our condition. We can spend more time in prayer for others. If we can stay on top of it and remain cheerful, we will encourage others who suffer.

How can we raise our children? Keep them in church. Encourage them to read the Bible as soon as they learn to read. Get them excited about prayer. God delights to answer the requests of children. Teach them to give. At times, God will use a child to win others to Christ.

What can we do about grown children? Put them in the Lord's hands when they leave home. Trust God to watch over them. Do not worry and fret; pray for them.

Have we ever come out of church and discover some thug ruined our tires? Perhaps we encounter some other problem. What can you do? One time our two front tires were slashed. Our friend drove across the city and brought us tires better than the slashed ones. He accepted no pay. If this happens to you, pray and ask God what to do. He helps those who seek to do right. Then when relief comes, thank and praise the Lord.

Has our child ever played hooky? Did our child say, "Mom, sign a note saying that I am sick." What did we do? One mother told the principal, "My child signed her own note. She did not stay home sick." In his office she told him where the girls went on that day. Later, the Captain opened the way to witness to the other mother. What will we do if our child skips school? Do not be too proud to admit the truth.

How can we build good character in our kids? Listen to them no matter what the importance of what they say. Let it be important to you. Take time with them and do not rush this. Time zooms by and children seem to grow up fast. Pray for our grown children. If they do something that displeases us, sometimes, we may rebuke them gently. Do not repeat it. Show them you love them without overindulging them.

Give the Helm to Jesus

Did our child ever call us godly? I remember how good it made me feel when my daughter called me godly, though I felt unworthy of this term. "The highway of the upright *is* to depart from evil: he that keepeth his way preserveth his soul" (Prov. 16:17). May we become women with a godly character.

Stay in the Word of God and have regular times of prayer. Then apply the Word to your life as Ellen did. This is the highway of a woman of integrity.

Endnote

1 "Her Hobby Is Helping" by Lynn Wallace in *God's Special People*, July 1992, pages 7-9.

Bibliography

Armitage, Vernon, and Mark Littleton, *Living Life to the Max,* Barbour Publishing: Uhrichsville OH, 2004.

Hanks, Scott, *The Men of Proverbs.* Independent Baptist Books: Pinellas Park, Florida.

Henry, Matthew, *Matthew Henry's Commentary,* vols. 1-6 (Wordsearch)

Ironside, H. A., *Ironside Commentaries: Proverbs.* Lifeline Printing, 1996.

Mayhall, Carol, *Lord of my Rocking Boat.* Pinon Press, 1998.

Mayhue, Richard, *Practicing Proverbs: Wise Living for Foolish Times.*Christian Focus Publications: Scotland UK, 2004.

McGee, J. Vernon, *Thru the Bible Commentary: Proverbs.* Nelsonword Publishing Group: 1993.

Olford, Stephen, *Windows of Wisdom: Devotional Studies in Proverbs.* Ambassador International: Greenville SC, and Belfast, Ireland, 2004.

Phillips, John, *Exploring Proverbs,* Vols. 1 & 2. Kregel Publications: Grand Rapids MI, 2002.

Wiersbe, *Be Skillful (Proverbs), The Be Series.* David C. Cook: Colorado Springs CO, 1995.